cycling in sussex

off-road trails & quiet Lanes   deirdre Huston & marina Bullivant

VERTEBRATE PUBLISHING

Design and production by Vertebrate Publishing, Sheffield.

www.v-publishing.co.uk

cycling in sussex

off-road trails & quiet lanes   deirdre huston & marina bullivant

ISBN: 978-1-906148-07-2

All photography by Deirdre Huston, except page 83, by Anthony Brown, and pages 77 & 108, by www.istockphoto.com

Edited by John Coefield
Vertebrate Publishing
www.**v-publishing**.co.uk

Mixed Sources
Product group from well-managed
forests and other controlled sources
www.fsc.org Cert no. SGS-COC-003963
© 1996 Forest Stewardship Council

FSC

contents

INTRODUCTION

We've had a brilliant time exploring Sussex in our quest for quality cycle rides and we hope you enjoy riding them as much as we have. This guide gives you a choice of twenty circular routes all of which are a mix of quiet lanes and off-road bridleways. They'll take you off the beaten track and help you avoid the honeypots, giving you an enticing and enduring glimpse of rural Sussex.

We both have families of our own and so we've included a section of particularly short routes ideal for adventurous families. There are also sections telling you about Railway Trails and Seafront Trails that are suitable for cyclists of all ages and abilities. The main routes aren't all easy and they're not all hard. Most are somewhere in between,

depending on the weather and the speed and style in which you cycle. If you don't want to ride up a hill, you can push and if you want to speed your heart rate up, you can pedal faster.

Ride the routes at your own pace and in your own way but whatever else you do, enjoy yourselves. It's hard not to when you're cycling through the Weald or beneath the Downs. Sussex must be one of the most beautiful counties in England and there's plenty of stunning countryside just waiting to be explored.

Enjoy riding in Sussex. Happy cycling!
Deirdre Huston & Marina Bullivant

Farnham

A31

A3

A286

A272

B2146

B2141

South
Downs

Chichester

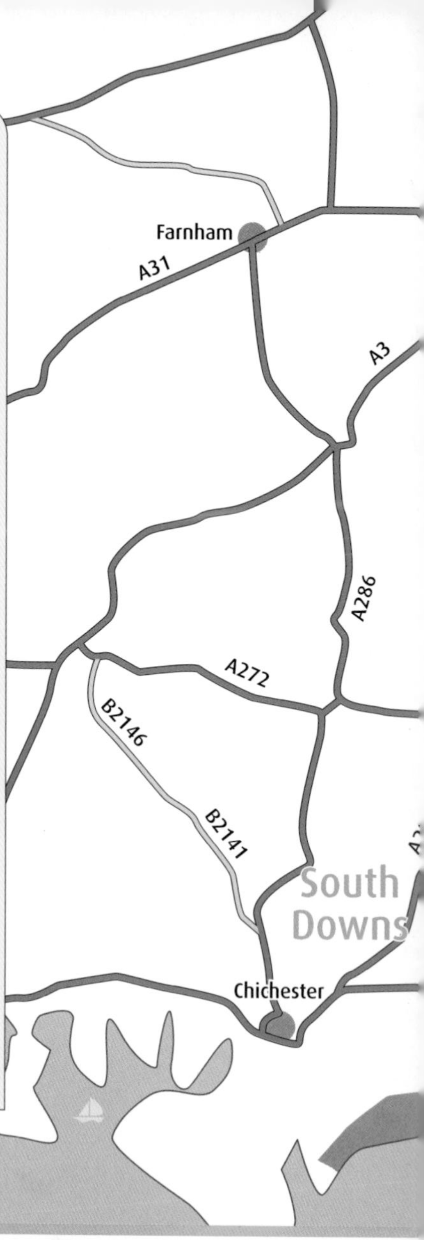

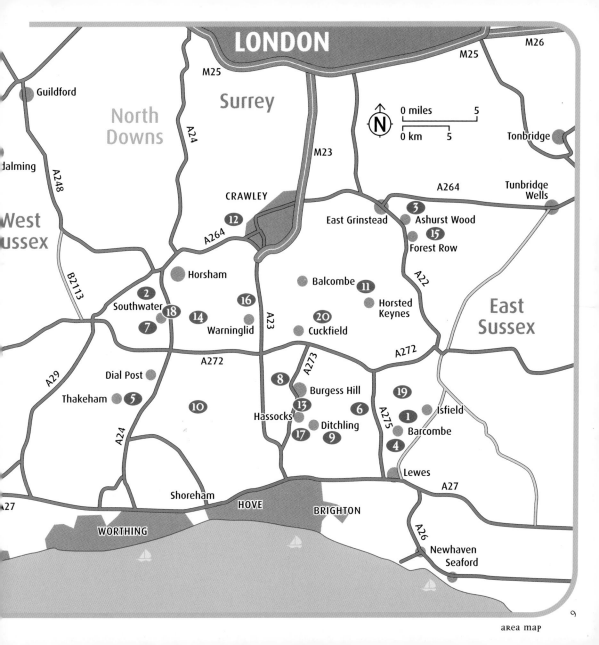

area map

acknowledgements

Thanks to the following people who have all contributed their help either by route-testing, allowing themselves to be photographed or by offering support: Julie Blackham, John, Magda and Pete Bullivant, Liz Grimes, Bob and Olive Huston, Karen Noble, James and Julie Purvis, Danny and Sarah Lessacher, Ian, Rory, Sean and Tegan Rayland, Nicky Rowe, Carol Turner, Rebecca Turner and Andy Waring.

We know we sometimes ask a lot of our friends and family: mud, hills, more broken bikes than you would think possible and no time to stop at the pub. Many thanks, especially for keeping on smiling and making us laugh.

a note on the rides

This book is aimed at novice and intermediate riders. The sections on **Railway Trails** and **Seafront Trails** are a good place to start as they promise flat, easy cycling. If you're riding with children, consider the short family rides which offer small slices of cycling adventure. These are also great walks and a good introduction for those new to off-road cycling.

The main routes are all circular offering a mix of quiet lanes, off-road bridleways and perhaps a section of a railway trail here and there. Each circuit has its own character and will alter depending on the season. Some have a significant amount of off-road and others are mainly on hard surfaces. We've included optional routes where appropriate so that you can tailor a ride to your own likes and dislikes. There are also digressions to pubs or places of interest.

It's surprising how many quiet roads there are in Sussex and these circuits avoid traffic wherever possible. The bridleways vary enormously in terms of surface and soil. The weather, ground condition and your own tolerance for mud will have a huge impact on how hard a ride is. All off-road sections will be more rideable in dry weather. We've tested a lot of these routes through the winter so don't let our references to puddles and mud put you off. The routes are ordered by difficulty with the easier routes at the front. The early routes give you the chance to try short off-road sections, sometimes offering road alternatives. As the routes progress, we include more off-road and the circuits tend to be longer. The routes at the back have harder off-road sections with some uphill climbs, steeper on-road hills and/or more mileage.

Note that central Sussex is a mix of sandstone, clay and chalk. The area around Burgess Hill and south of Horsham is Weald clay. All clay can be heavy and has a nasty habit of sticking to your bike. This guide covers central Sussex, stretching from Seaford to Worthing, from Forest Row to Barns Green. Many of the circuits have breathtaking views of the Downs and Weald without actually venturing up those gradients onto the Downs themselves. The one exception is the short Jack and Jill route where you can give the Downs a try. In general the routes don't include hills unless they're in the way and we've aimed to put climbs on easier surfaces wherever possible.

The rides are circular, starting and finishing at appropriate parking or public transport facilities. We offer plenty of suggestions for pubs or cafes, adding useful detail where possible.

maps, descriptions, distances

While every effort has been made to ensure accuracy within the maps and descriptions in this guide, things change and we are unable to guarantee that every detail is correct. Treat stated distances as guidelines. We strongly recommend that you carry a detailed map of the area with you when riding and do not rely solely on this guide. A 'proper' map will provide more information and help you find your way if you get lost and ride off the maps included here.

your bike

Any bike will get you round the easier routes in this book, provided it works. If you're going to venture off-road, we'd recommend a mountain bike, as the increased toughness and comfort will pay dividends. To an extent, the more you pay, the more fun you'll have, if only because very cheap bikes are heavy and unreliable.

Check that everything works – you won't be going anywhere fast if your gears seize, but you'll probably be a little quicker than planned if your brakes fail... Pump the tyres up, check they aren't about to wear through and ensure that everything that should be tight is tight. If you're not sure you can do this yourself, visit your local bike shop.

clothing

You need to get your clothing right if you want to stay comfortable on a bike, especially in bad weather.

Ideally, you should choose clothing made from 'technical' synthetic or wool fabrics which 'wick' or draw the sweat away from your body and then dry quickly, preventing you from getting cold and damp. Stay away from cotton, as it absorbs moisture and then holds onto it, becoming heavy, uncomfortable and cold. If it's chilly, wear a layer of thin fleece on top to keep you warm, and then a wind/waterproof on top of this, to keep out the elements.

As cycling is an active sport, it's worth setting off just a little on the cool side as you'll soon warm up on the first hill. Don't leave the warm clothes behind though, as the weather could turn and they'll keep you warm on lunch stops.

If the ground is wet and you're going off-road, wear shoes that have good grip and will keep out the mud and any water.

gloves

Cycling gloves help prevent blisters and numb hands and keep your fingers warm. They also provide a surprising amount of protection if you fall off.

route map key

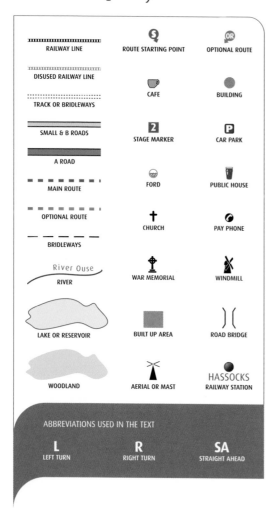

▦▦▦▦▦▦▦▦ RAILWAY LINE	⚑ ROUTE STARTING POINT	OR OPTIONAL ROUTE
▨▨▨▨▨▨▨▨ DISUSED RAILWAY LINE		
⋯⋯⋯⋯⋯⋯⋯ TRACK OR BRIDLEWAYS	☕ CAFE	● BUILDING
━━━━━━ SMALL & B ROADS	2 STAGE MARKER	P CAR PARK
━━━━━━ A ROAD		
▬ ▬ ▬ ▬ MAIN ROUTE	🕶 FORD	🍺 PUBLIC HOUSE
▬ ▬ ▬ ▬ OPTIONAL ROUTE	✝ CHURCH	☏ PAY PHONE
⎯ ⎯ ⎯ BRIDLEWAYS		
River Ouse ⎯⎯ RIVER	⚰ WAR MEMORIAL	🎠 WINDMILL
LAKE OR RESERVOIR	▣ BUILT UP AREA	)(ROAD BRIDGE
WOODLAND	⚕ AERIAL OR MAST	● HASSOCKS RAILWAY STATION

ABBREVIATIONS USED IN THE TEXT

L	R	SA
LEFT TURN	RIGHT TURN	STRAIGHT AHEAD

other essentials

Take any necessary spare parts for your bike, tools and a pump. We'd suggest taking a spare inner tube, as it's far quicker to swop tubes than to stop and repair a puncture. Be aware that children's bikes may have smaller wheels than yours and may need different tubes! Also consider spare clothes, a first aid kit and make sure you have enough food and water.

You'll need something to carry this little lot in. We'd suggest a rucksack as many are now compatible with water bladders which allow you to drink on the move via a tube and mouthpiece. Panniers, on the other hand, keep the weight off you and on your bike, although they can bounce around and make the bike unwieldy on rough ground. Whatever you choose, make sure it's big enough to carry everything, including any excess clothing you may be wearing.

rights of way

Countryside access in the UK hasn't been particularly kind to cyclists, although things are improving. We have 'right of way' on bridleways (blue arrows on signs) and byways (red arrows). However, having 'right of way' doesn't actually mean having **the** right of way, just that we're allowed to ride there – so give way to walkers and horse riders. We're also allowed to ride on green lanes and some unclassified roads, although the only way to determine which are legal and which aren't is to check with the local countryside authority.

Everything else – footpaths, open countryside and so forth is, sadly, out of bounds.

rules of the (off) road

- Always ride on legal trails.
- Ride considerately – give way to horses and pedestrians.
- Don't spook animals.
- Ride in control – you don't know who's around the next corner.
- Leave gates as you find them – if you're unsure, shut them.
- Keep the noise down and don't swear loudly when you fall off in front of walkers.
- Leave no trace – take home everything you took out.
- Keep water sources clean – don't take toilet stops near streams.
- Enjoy the countryside and respect its life and work.

general safety
(a.k.a. 'common sense')

Cycling can be dangerous. Too much exuberance on a descent in the middle of nowhere could leave you in more than a spot of bother. Consider your limitations and relative fragility before launching at something.

Carry food and water, spares, a tube and pump. Consider a first-aid kit. Even if it's warm, the weather could turn, so take a wind/waterproof. Think about what could happen on an enforced stop. Pack lights if you could finish in the dark, as over-ambitious family trips often do.

The ability to map-read, navigate and understand weather warnings is essential. Don't go out in bad weather unless you're confident and capable of doing so.

While these routes keep to quiet lanes as much as is possible, roads in this region can be very busy. Plan accordingly, obey the Highway Code and assume the majority of drivers are idiots...

If riding alone, think about the potential seriousness of an accident – you could be without help for a long time. Tell someone where you're going and when you'll be back. Take a phone if you have one, but don't rely on getting a signal. (And don't call an ambulance because you've grazed your knee.)

Riding in a group is safer (ambitious overtaking manoeuvres excepted) and often more fun, but don't leave slower riders behind and give them a breather when they've caught up.

When choosing your route, check the weather, the amount of daylight/time available and the ability/experience of each rider. Allow more time than you think necessary to allow for problems.

Always ride in control and give way to others, especially on popular routes. Bells might be annoying, but they work. If you can't bring yourself to bolt one on, a polite 'excuse me' should be fine.

On hot, sunny days, make sure that you slap some Factor 30+ and **ALWAYS WEAR YOUR HELMET!**

the routes

The first three routes are designed for families with children who are confident on two wheels. If you want to have a go at riding on a mix of surfaces in a circular route, these are a good place to start. The River Ouse Family Route is a real find as it should be fairly easy to cycle most of the year. Children will find the other two are more challenging in terms of terrain and slopes but it gives them the chance to be adventurous and explore off-road bridleways. We've ridden them with children as young as six and seven but as children vary so much, please read the introduction to each route before you decide if it's suitable for your family.

If you have baby seats, tag-alongs, stabilisers and pre-school children in tow, turn straight to the sections on Railway Trails (page 132) and Seafront Trails (page 138) which offer flat, easy riding.

With a focus on the central area of Sussex, the remainder of the routes allow you to explore one of the most beautiful counties in Britain. Leafy lanes, off-road trails and ancient bridleways link up to form original routes. Gradually increasing in difficulty through the book, these routes will take you through rural idylls, past fine agricultural countryside, swooping down deserted country lanes and past many of the treasures Sussex has to offer: windmills, the Weald, the Channel... Enjoy!

RIVER OUSE family route

BARCOMBE MILLS // ISFIELD

ROUTE 1 // 4km (2.5 MILES)

This route is short, safe and fun. It combines parts of Routes 4 and 19, but it's such a great family route that we've decided to make life easy for you and put it in as a route in its own right. It's the ideal family introduction to cycling, with easy, level off-road tracks and lots to see. You are cycling to The Anchor Inn by the River Ouse where you can either walk into the nearby fields to picnic on the riverbank or indulge in some high-quality pub food and drink.

You can also hire rowing boats from the pub, which always makes for an interesting, if not magical, family experience. You may want to save up first though as it can be pricey.

You can extend the route by riding on towards Isfield on our **Optional Route**. This second section is also off-road. It's mainly level but the ground underfoot is rougher. It is easy enough for older families in summer but when conditions are wet, it will best suit mud-lovers and comfortable off-road cyclists.

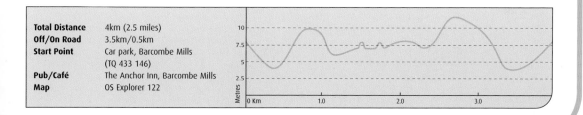

Total Distance	4km (2.5 miles)
Off/On Road	3.5km/0.5km
Start Point	Car park, Barcombe Mills
	(TQ 433 146)
Pub/Café	The Anchor Inn, Barcombe Mills
Map	OS Explorer 122

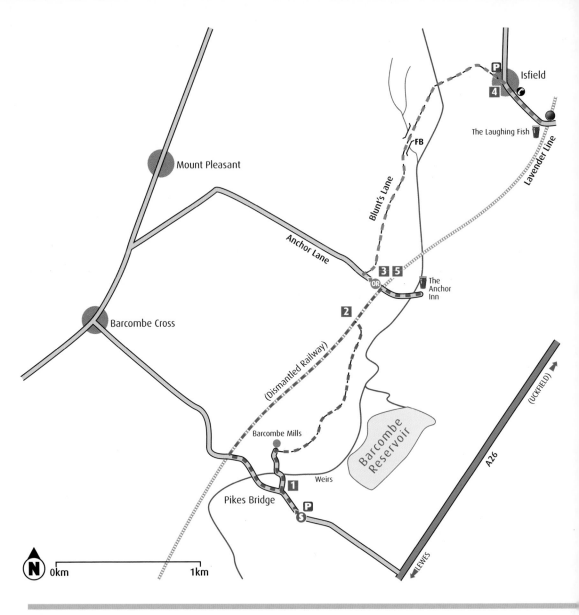

Mount Pleasant

Anchor Lane

Blunt's Lane

FB

Isfield

P

4

The Laughing Fish

Lavender Line

3 5

OR

The Anchor Inn

Barcombe Cross

2

(Dismantled Railway)

Barcombe Reservoir

Barcombe Mills

Weirs

1

Pikes Bridge

P
S

(UCKFIELD)

A26

LEWES

N

0km   1km

Starting point: Driving from Barcombe Cross, sweep painlessly down the hill in your car and cross the bridge. There's a car park on the left, just after the Environment Agency sign at the entrance to Barcombe Mills. Alternatively, if you're driving from Lewes/Uckfield on the A26, turn off near Clayhill Nurseries towards Barcombe Mills. The car park is on your right before the bridge.

Alternative Starting Point – Isfield Post Office:
See **Optional Route** (Instruction 4).

Turn **R** out of the car park.

1 At the Environment Agency sign, turn **R** where it says Weak Bridge. This is the access road to Barcombe Mills. Take the time to have a look around if you can. It's a little bit different. After the weir by the old toll bridge, go **SA**.

Cycle up the unmade road through the houses until just past the converted barn, where you must turn **R**. Cycle round the metal gate and continue **SA**. Cross a small bridge over the River Ouse, continuing along this easy bridleway until you see a red-tiled bungalow with a slate roof ahead. There's a choice of footpaths here. You need to take the one to the far **L**. The waymarker is next to the telegraph pole with the yellow warning triangle. Follow the track that leads beside the red bungalow. **Please dismount and push your bike on this very short stretch through the trees**.

2 Go through a gate and **immediately**, turn **R**. Cycle along the muddy track, which is a bridleway. You are following the path of a dismantled railway. Initially there's no evidence of this but children can look out for two signs of the trains that used to run here: the railway bridge and the old rails embedded in Anchor Lane. Manoeuvre your bikes over the sleepers and past the gate.

Local knowledge

Historically, Barcombe Mills was an important navigational route and milling location. This has resulted in the complex network of islands and channels that you can see today. Site-owner, the Environment Agency, is trying to encourage rough grassland, scrub and hedgerow to develop in order to improve the habitats on offer for birds, invertebrates, small mammals, bats, reptiles and amphibians. Children are unlikely to spot most of the above but they might want to look for the tollgate sign and the weir.

food and drink

The Anchor Inn boasts a riverside location, good Harveys, high-quality food and some magical rowing boats.

3 You are now on Anchor Lane. It's beautiful but can be narrow with occasional traffic so you might want to get children to push their bikes. Turn **R** to reach the food, beer and rowing boats on offer at The Anchor Inn. It's worth noting that this pub is popular in high season and this lane will be busier at weekends in particular as a result. After you've explored the river and/or pub, return along Anchor Lane to find the bridleway on your **L**. The main route continues at Instruction 5.

Optional Route (adds approx. 3km)

Turn **L** and cycle for a short distance along Anchor Lane, ignoring the small footbridge off to the right. Ride **R** at the wooden waymarker post. Go through the gate and follow the track along the line of the fence. Ignore any gaps in the hedge. Where the grass widens, keep right, heading towards the (currently broken) gateway. There's a faded bridleway marker on the wooden gatepost. Continue cycling with the hedge on your right and the fence on your left. Where the track opens out onto the field, you can see a WWII pill box ahead. Cycle **SA**, keeping the pill box close on your left to avoid the wettest ground. Follow the track towards two large oaks and ride on to where the track disappears into the trees at the corner of the field. Go through the gate and if it's muddy, skid down and up this dipping section of bridleway. Just make sure you don't end up in the stream. Pass across the wooden bridge (with gates at both ends). Looking across the field, you can just see a gate some way to the left of the house. Bump along the bridleway across this grass in the direction of the gate. Pass through the gate and ride over another wooden bridge, following the bridleway **SA**.

4 At the end of the bridleway, you have a choice: turn back now or turn **R** onto the road and cycle a few hundred metres to The Laughing Fish pub or The Lavender Line.

Immediately to the left of the bridleway end is Isfield Post Office, housed in a utility-looking building. There's parking here if you wish to use Isfield as an alternative starting point.

To return to Anchor Lane, retrace your steps: Cross back over the wooden bridge and go through the gate and keep to the bridleway cycling diagonally left across the open field towards the bridge ahead. Go through the metal gate, across the wooden bridge and through the gate on the far side. Keep **SA** on Blunt's Lane bridleway with the River Ouse on your left. After a short slope emerge from the trees onto a field. Cycle past the oak trees. Go round the WWII pill box, keeping it on your right to avoid the wettest ground. After the pill box, look right through the trees to find the track which runs **SA** along the hedge and fence. Keep riding **SA** between the hedge and the fence. Pass through a gateway. Ride through the clearing, keeping **SA** with the hedge on your left. Cycle along this grassy bridleway that is bordered by hedges. On reaching a small field keep to the right, until you reach a gate that leads you onto Anchor Lane. Ride **L** and look out for the bridleway where you need to turn **R**.

5 Make your return back along the path of the dismantled railway but this time, ignore the footpath by the bungalow. Instead, ride **SA** towards Barcombe Mills on the bridleway, ignoring any footpaths or farm tracks. Some sections have been coated with chalk to improve the surface. Towards the end, the sides rise up steeply. Upon reaching the road opposite The Ticket Office turn **L**. There's a very short stretch of road cycling and you can push if you want to. Look out for the footpath leading in front of the houses that will take you back through Barcombe Mills, avoiding the road as you return to your car.

BARNS GREEN MINI-CIRCUIT

ROUTE 2 // 4.8km (3 miLes)

This is a route in miniature. We're always on the lookout for short routes that are ideal for beginners or those with smaller children, but believe it or not, the fact that they're short makes them much harder to find. And they always seem to have a rush-hour road running through the middle of them. But not this one.

We happened upon it almost by accident when testing a nearby route. There are no busy roads in this circuit, the off-road section is bumpy and fun but not too arduous and any manageable uphill pushes will soon be forgotten in the downhill run back to the car.

This circuit is ideal for a family who want to see how their kids will cope with some gentle cycling challenges. The muddy nature of the off-road sections means that it's probably best to go when the ground is dry. The route also includes one or two spots that look ripe for a picnic. And of course, there's always The Queen's Head in Barns Green if you fancy a post-ride drink.

The route starts from the car parks near Barns Green recreation ground. Barns Green is between Horsham, Southwater and Billingshurst and the village is signed from most surrounding roads. Heading south on the Itchingfield-Billingshurst road (Plumtree Cross Lane) look out for the crossroads signed to Muntham House School in front of the village sign and football pitch. After turning right, the first hall on the right is Barns Green Village Club and the second is the village hall. Pick your parking with care; some is restricted.

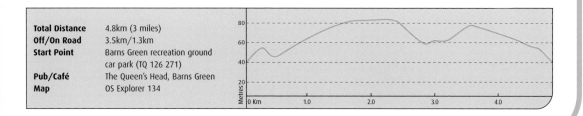

Total Distance	4.8km (3 miles)	
Off/On Road	3.5km/1.3km	
Start Point	Barns Green recreation ground car park (TQ 126 271)	
Pub/Café	The Queen's Head, Barns Green	
Map	OS Explorer 134	

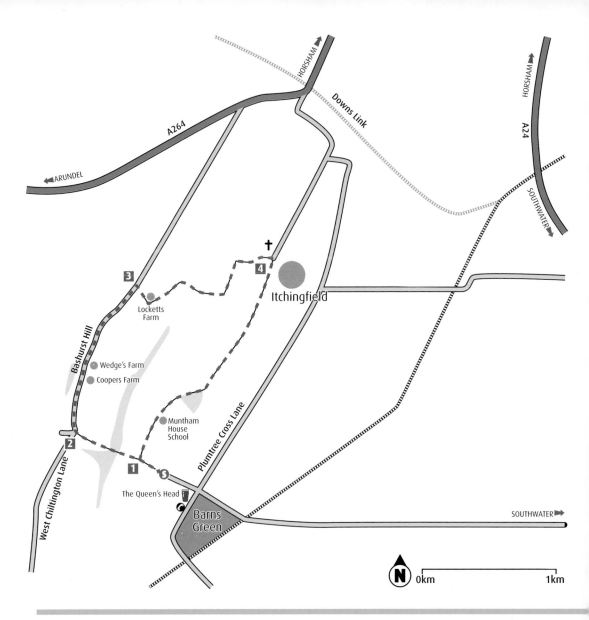

HORSHAM

Downs Link

HORSHAM

A264

A24

ARUNDEL

SOUTHWATER

3

Bashurst Hill

Locketts Farm

Wedge's Farm

Coopers Farm

✝

4

Itchingfield

Muntham House School

Plumtree Cross Lane

West Chiltington Lane

2

1

The Queen's Head

Barns Green

SOUTHWATER ➡

N 0km 1km

Follow the lane past the village hall and up a slight gradient. You will pass the entrance to Muntham House School on your right. At the top of the hill, follow the lane as it curves round. Owlets House is on your right and a leafy bridleway forks left.

1 Ride **L** down the bridleway. Watch out for large stones and potholes on the descent. Go through a gate and **SA** across a field. This is a deceptive uphill that does require some muscle power. You'll pass a wooden waymarked sign on your right and the bridleway will turn into a compacted stone path.

2 Go through a metal gate and turn **R** onto the lane. Take care; you're on the only road section of the route. This gradual uphill should be manageable for most. Pass Guildings, Coopers Barn, Coopers Farm, The Coopers and ride on. Notice the red post box at Wedge's Farm, and ride on past Rapleys and The Wedges. Pass Shiprods Farm on your left. If you're tempted by the farm produce, the farm is a short ride up the drive. Pass gateposts for Shiprods Manor on the left and a footpath on your right. Look out for Locketts Farm. Soon after it, you'll see a wooden waymarked bridleway on the right.

3 Turn **R** here. Go through the narrow entrance and ride downhill passing beside Locketts Farm. You'll come to a gate. To avoid this, go **SA** from the gate across the top of the field. Any child who can spot the hidden bridleway sign will be doing well. Pass through the gap into a second big field. You need to go **SA** and then **R**, following the bridleway around the edge of the field. Towards the corner of the field, it turns into a narrow track that disappears into the trees. Keep going, passing through the gate and cycle along a bridleway running between two wire and post fences with fields on both sides. Go through a gap which leads into another field. Follow the

famILy RIDING

Young families might want to head for Southwater Country Park. There's an easy-to-cycle track which leads around a lake. In the summer you'll often see sailing dinghies, canoes and windsurfers enjoying the water. There's an adventure-style play area and a wildlife area. The park can be accessed without going on any roads from Southwater Cycles hire shop; on leaving the shop, head for the shiny silver bicycles opposite and turn **L**. If you want to hire a trailer-bike, you'll need to book in advance.

wooden waymarked sign **L** along the track and round the edge of the field. The bridleway leads through a gate and into a copse where there's a fairly sudden, steep-ish slope down towards a wooden bridge and up the other side. Follow the bridleway sign to the right up towards the small gate. Go through and head diagonally across the field towards the five-bar gate. If you look back, you should see the church over your left shoulder.

4 When you pass through the gate, you will see Itchingfield Primary School opposite. Take a sharp **R** up the bridleway/lane past the metal half-gate. There is an uphill section here but you can tell the children that once you reach the top, it will be downhill all the way back to the car. Look out for some imposing gateposts with stone-carved rams' skulls and the cottage with the gothic door and windows. Go **SA** through the gate. From now on, it's plain sailing. Follow the bridleway as it bears right. You will pass through Muntham Home Farm. The farmhouse is on your right and the coach house is on your left. You might recognise Owlets on your left and the leafy bridleway you took at the start of the circuit. Cycle around the bend, past Muntham House School and back to your car.

ashurst wood
mini mountain bike circuit
route 3 // 5.6km (3.5 miles)

There are two things which make this route suitable for children and/or adults interested in trying off-road cycling: the short mileage and the fact that it's all bridleways, the majority of which are relatively smooth. That said, there are also mud, grass and stony tracks plus a number of hills to contend with and children do need to be confident on two wheels. Gears and long trousers might help too.

One stony downhill stands out as tricky and requires bike-pushing or a sensible approach. Children who are accomplished cyclists will probably enjoy the challenge. One thing's for sure – the route's short enough that you can be confident of reaching the end, especially if you checked your brakes and tyres before setting out. But then again, with children in tow, nothing can be taken for granted...

The starting point is along Hammerwood Road in Ashurst Wood. Coming from Forest Row on the A22, take the right fork for Ashurst Wood (Wall Hill Road) and then the first turning on the right (Hammerwood Road – the first section is one-way). Look out for the layby on the left-hand side of the road in front of some houses.

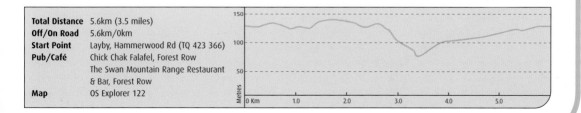

Total Distance	5.6km (3.5 miles)
Off/On Road	5.6km/0km
Start Point	Layby, Hammerwood Rd (TQ 423 366)
Pub/Café	Chick Chak Falafel, Forest Row
	The Swan Mountain Range Restaurant & Bar, Forest Row
Map	OS Explorer 122

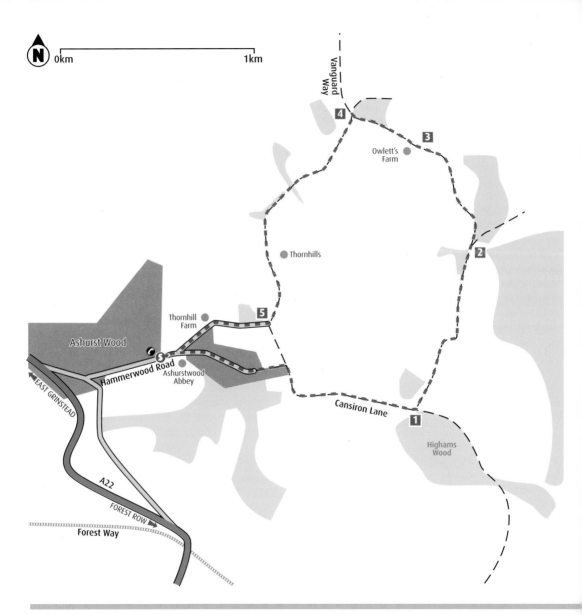

N

0km 1km

Vanguard
Way

4

3

Owlett's
Farm

Thornhills

2

Thornhill
Farm

5

Ashurst Wood

S

Hammerwood Road

Ashurstwood
Abbey

EAST GRINSTEAD

A22

FOREST ROW

Forest Way

Cansiron Lane

1

Highams
Wood

Set off east along Hammerwood Road, passing Ashurstwood Abbey and School Lane. When you see the post-box ahead, take the **R** fork down Cansiron Lane. This is a bridleway, but the tarmac surface makes for easy riding. Continue **SA**, ignoring a footpath that passes in front of you. The lane bends around to the right and slowly climbs. Adults may not notice the slope but children will. Pass Blackberry Hill Farm on your right and Orchard Cottages on your left

1 At the entrance to Highams Wood, go **L** and keep cycling as the bridleway becomes stonier. Where the track bends to the right, pause to take in the view across the fields. The path continues through the trees and narrows with encroaching undergrowth. As you pedal downhill, the bridleway widens. As you approach the wood, stop at the farm gate to admire the striking form of two dead trees rooted before the rural backdrop of Owlett's Farm.

2 At the fork, ride **L** through the five-bar gate. The next section of the circuit requires caution, as the brick surface is rather uneven. There's plenty of time to get used to the surface before the final steep descent. Budding mountain bikers can demonstrate their skill by keeping their pedals level. More cautious riders can dismount and push. Don't risk taking the slope too fast – you don't want to end up in the farmyard sooner than you expected!

3 Pass **SA** through two more farm gates and notice the intriguing sculpture in the garden of Owlett's Farmhouse. If places have atmospheres, this valley has a tranquil but friendly feel to it. Whilst it's tempting to stop a while, you do have to climb back up the other side and, as some would argue, the sooner the better. As you bear right up through the middle of the farm buildings, your party may divide into those who want to take it slow and those who want to go for the burn. If you're one of the

Local Knowledge
This route is known locally as 'The Large Triangle' and rumour has it that the two dead trees were struck by lightning. Let's hope the only lightning you'll see will be the speed of your children's bikes.

food & drink
Nearby Forest Row and Ashurst Wood offer some interesting shopping and eating experiences including the friendly bike hire shop. See our **Forest Row** route on page 97 for details.

making a day of it
You could always take a linear route along Forest Way after lunch (see **Forest Row** on page 97 for start point).

latter, why don't you see if you can make it all the way to the top without stopping? The lane levels out. Pass the well-named Dog Gate House on your left and Dog Gate Lodge on your right.

4 Notice where the bridleway is signed **L** and turn to cycle along Vanguard Way. This part of the ride is very gently uphill. Pass Songhurst on the left. Enjoy a short bumpy freewheel before another slight uphill. Pass Hurstbrook House and Thornhills on your left. Hear the gravel crunch under your wheels as you ride between the post and rail fences towards Homefield Cottage on your left.

5 Turn **R** and whiz down the concrete lane. There's one last short uphill that takes you past Thornhill Farm and Mouse Hall. Continue **SA** to the junction at Hammerwood Road and return to the start.

Lewes villages
& the RIVER OUSE

COOKSBRIDGE // BARCOMBE MILLS // ANCHOR INN // BARCOMBE

ROUTE 4 // 15.3km (9.5 miles)

It's hard not to like this route. It meanders through the Sussex countryside, allowing you to explore ancient Barcombe Mills and develop the equally ancient art of relaxing on the riverside with a pint. If at least one person in your party is feeling energetic, you can even hire a rowing boat and drift downstream. The Anchor Inn also crops up in the Chailey circuit but the two routes are completely different.

This is a good route for when the ground is wet, with the majority of the circuit being on quiet country lanes or bridleways with a good hard surface. In very wet weather, it's good to know that any boggy sections are short enough to push your bike over or through the mud. If you want to bring your bike by train, Cooksbridge station is located conveniently opposite the starting point. Alternatively, drive into Cooksbridge on the A275 and park in Chandlers Mead, opposite H's Café by Cooksbridge Station.

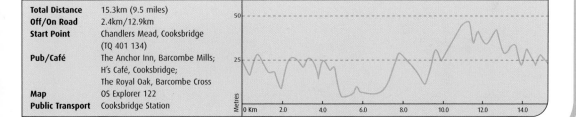

Total Distance	15.3km (9.5 miles)
Off/On Road	2.4km/12.9km
Start Point	Chandlers Mead, Cooksbridge (TQ 401 134)
Pub/Café	The Anchor Inn, Barcombe Mills; H's Café, Cooksbridge; The Royal Oak, Barcombe Cross
Map	OS Explorer 122
Public Transport	Cooksbridge Station

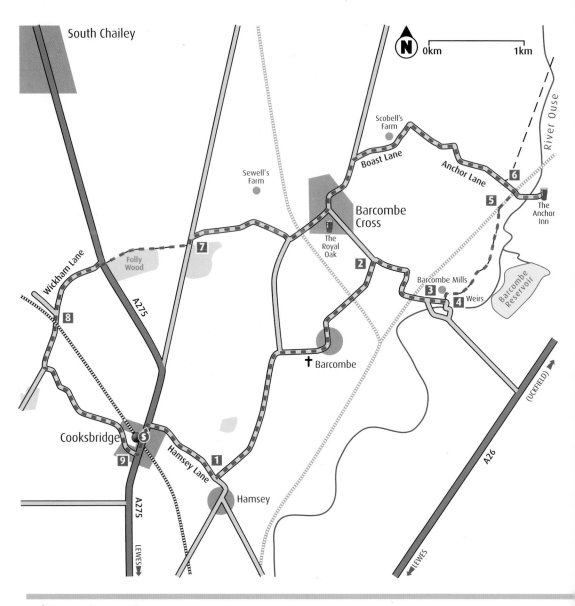

South Chailey

N
0km   1km

River Ouse

Scobell's
Farm

Boast Lane   Anchor Lane

Sewell's
Farm

6

5

The
Anchor
Inn

Barcombe
Cross

The Royal
Oak   **2**

Wickham Lane   **7**   Folly
Wood

Barcombe Mills   Barcombe
Reservoir

3   **4** Weirs

A275

8

✝ Barcombe

(UCKFIELD)

Cooksbridge   S   A26

9   **1**

Hamsey Lane

Hamsey

A275   LEWES   LEWES

Cycle **R** out of Chandlers Mead onto an almost-too-short-to-mention section of the A275. Turn **R**, following the sign for Hamsey. Continue cycling along Hamsey Lane.

1 At the T-junction, cycle **L** towards Barcombe on this up and down lane. At the white signpost, turn **R** for Barcombe Mills. Pass the church and follow the wall round as the road curves. Ignore the lane on your left opposite the post box. Carry on cycling over the bridge and up the hill.

2 Turn **R** at the T-junction, towards Barcombe Mills. This lane offers some wide open views and a steep, sweeping downhill. Let your wheels spin as you look right to spot the old site of the The Anglers Rest pub and the ticket office.

3 As you approach the bridge, turn **L** into the lane. Mill Farm is in front of you. Pedal on down the lane.

NB: The access road to Barcombe Mills is on your right. Take the time to have a look around if you can; it's a little bit different. Note in particular the weir by the old toll bridge.

4 Cycle **L** up the unmade road through the houses until just past the converted barn; turn **R** here. Cycle around the metal gate and continue **SA**. Cross a small bridge over the River Ouse, continuing along this easy bridleway until you see a red-tiled bungalow with a slate roof ahead.

There is a choice of footpaths here: you need to take the one to the far **L**. The waymarker is next to the telegraph pole with the yellow warning triangle. Follow the track that leads beside the red bungalow. **Please dismount and push your bike on this very short stretch of the route through the trees.**

LOCAL KNOWLEDGE

Historically, Barcombe Mills was an important navigational route and milling location. This has resulted in the complex network of islands and channels that you can see today. The Environment Agency is trying to encourage rough grassland, scrub and hedgerow to develop in order to improve the habitats on offer for birds, invertebrates, small mammals, bats, reptiles and amphibians.

FOOD & DRINK

The Anchor Inn, Barcombe Mills is a riverside pub offering Harveys, high quality food and some magical rowing boats. **H's Café** in Cooksbridge serves food that fits the town's name. We can recommend the breakfasts if you like a good value, traditional café fry-up. Open Mon to Fri, 7am–2pm; Sat, 8am–12pm.

FAMILY RIDING

For a short, safe and fairly painless version of this route, check out our section for family rides (page 17).

5 Go through the gate. It takes you directly onto the muddy track that is a bridleway. Turn **R** and cycle along the bridleway. You are following the path of a dismantled railway although there is limited evidence of this. At the end, manoeuvre your bikes over the sleepers and past the gate.

6 You are now on Anchor Lane. It's beautiful but can be narrow with occasional traffic.

NB: Turn **R** to reach the food, beer and rowing boats on offer at The Anchor Inn. It's worth noting that this pub is very popular in high season and this lane will be particularly busy at weekends as a result.

Cycle **L** on Anchor Lane, past Delves Farm. The lane curves right at the post box and wends its way along past Scobell's Farm on the right. Use the passing places on offer.

At the end of Anchor Lane (a.k.a. Boast Lane) cycle **L** into Barcombe Cross over the bridge. Do your best to ignore the muscle crunching hill.

Continue **R** towards Lewes at the roundabout, pausing for thought and replenishment at The Royal Oak if you so desire. Cycle over the bridge that crosses the dismantled railway and follow the road to the right. Watch out for the camber at the side of the road because it's on easy stretches like this where you chat away and forget to look where you're going...

Pass a lane on your right to Sewell's Farm. Keep following the road as it leads you left. Look out for the 'Sublime to the Ridiculous' fancy dress shop.

7 At the T-junction, a fortunate few may spot a bridleway diagonally to the left. Otherwise, to find it, turn **L** as if heading towards Cooksbridge and almost immediately turn **R** leaving the road for the leafy bridleway. This wide bridleway enables you to choose your own path through the mud so that you may either enjoy the peaceful, rustling leaves of Folly Wood or the sound of your two wheels splashing and squelching through huge puddles.

Emerge onto the road and turn **R**. Almost straight away, go **L** at Wickham Lane. After a short uphill stretch, you are rewarded with a freewheeling downhill.

8 At the T-junction, ride **L**, following the white signpost towards Cooksbridge. Go under the railway. Continue cycling, ignoring the right turn on the bend after the little bridge. Pass the wind turbine at Cooksbridge recreation ground.

9 At the end of Beechwood Lane, cycle **L** back into Cooksbridge.

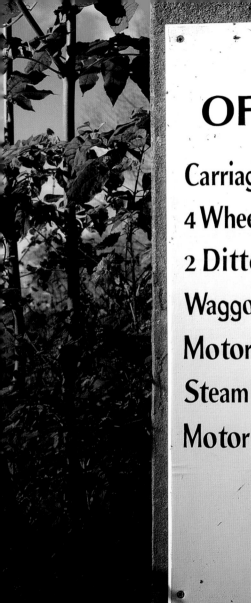

LIST
OF TOLLS

	s	d
Carriage & Horses	1	0
4 Wheels & 1 Horse		9
2 Ditto		6
Waggon & Horses	1	6
Motor Cars	1	0
Steam Engines	2	0
Motor & Side-Cars		3

RURaL IDyLLs

THakeHam // ASHINGtON

ROUte 5 // 14.5km (9 mILes)

You'll have to decide for yourself whether this route takes you through a rural idyll. You'll start with a chocolate box setting and get going with a rough ride on agricultural bridleways. Don't be put off because the middle part of the route is low on effort and high on enjoyment. Glide along easy bridleways through Sleepy Hollow, the place where Vera's dream drew breath, and gather pace on quiet lanes, slowing to take notice of the simple church at Warminghurst. Finish off your ride by exploring agricultural Sussex, taking care not to disturb the alpacas as you cycle along rural bridleways.

This ride offers a good taste of country life but those who don't like bumpy, muddy ground, some of which is on a slight incline, would be best to ride this in the summer. Those who enjoy making tyre tracks through puddles will enjoy it all year round.

Your starting point is in Thakeham. From the red post box on the B2133, turn into Cray's Lane. There's a layby on Cray's Lane opposite Cumberland House, near the church, where you may park.

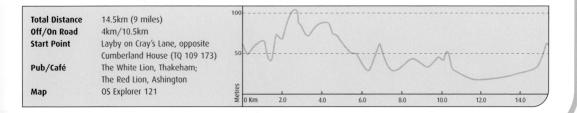

Total Distance	14.5km (9 miles)	
Off/On Road	4km/10.5km	
Start Point	Layby on Cray's Lane, opposite Cumberland House (TQ 109 173)	
Pub/Café	The White Lion, Thakeham; The Red Lion, Ashington	
Map	OS Explorer 121	

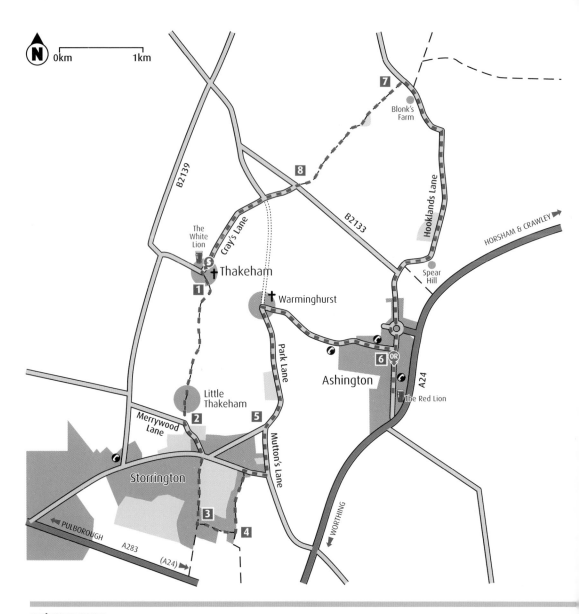

N
0km 1km

B2139

The White Lion
9
Cray's Lane
✝ Thakeham
1

7
Blonk's Farm

8

Hooklands Lane

B2133

HORSHAM & CRAWLEY

Spear Hill

✝ Warminghurst

Park Lane

Little Thakeham

Merrywood Lane
2
5

Storrington

Mutton's Lane

3
4

PULBOROUGH

A283

(A24)

Ashington

6 OR

A24

The Red Lion

WORTHING

Head south for the white Tudor-style house and turn **L** through the white gates along the bridleway.

1 Immediately after the cattle-grid, turn **R** and go up through the gate. Bump along the grassy track, following the bridleway sign. There's a distant tower to your right (an old brickworks?) and views back over Thakeham and on towards the South Downs. Pass through another gate and turn **R**, sticking to the bridleway.

After an occasionally-muddy downhill, the bridleway turns to concrete. Go through the middle gate, following the bridleway **SA** and pedal hard up past the huge rocks (or are they standing stones?). Continue **R** onto the tarmac lane.

2 Turn **L** onto Merrywood Lane. Soon, you'll hit a busy road. Cross with care to follow Hampers Lane bridleway **SA**. Stay on this easy bridleway (also used by cars accessing the houses) until you reach the red pillar box and parish council sign.

3 Turn **L** along Sanctuary Lane. You are now cycling through Longbury Hill Estate and Sleepy Hollow. Cycle **SA** past the phone box.

NB: By the red phone box, look out for Sanctuary Cottage and Vera's shelter (see **Local Knowledge** right).

4 Ride **L** down George's Lane. Pass Warren Hill (owned by the National Trust) on your right. Cycle onwards. Turn **R** into Rock Road and then where the road bends, turn **L** into Mutton's Lane. Flit down the hill and at the fork, cycle **R** for Ashington.

Local knowledge

Cycle through the site of a unique social experiment, an area now known as Sleepy Hollow. In 1922, Vera Pragnell, the 25 year old daughter of a textile magnate, bought 50 acres of land here. Her aim was to establish a commune where people of all classes could thrive as a community. Vera gave out plots of land and the 'settlers' built wooden shacks, grew vegetables and tended livestock. Conditions were basic but community spirits ran high and there was dancing on the green beside Vera's house (now Sanctuary Cottage beside the phone box). Scandal threatened when local papers carried salacious reports of 'free love' and naked frolicking. However, the community's eventual undoing appears to have been the lure of individual wealth as one-by-one, plots were sold off. Today, you can still see Vera's Shelter, a small reminder of Vera's dream.

food & drink

The White Lion has an idyllic setting in the village of Thakeham and is mentioned in the Good Beer Guide. **The Red Lion** in Ashington offers family dining.

5 At the top of Park Lane, come to Warminghurst Church. The fabric of the church building dates from circa 1220. Whether you're a churchgoer or not, the building is worth a quick look because it is beautiful in its simplicity.

Cycle **R** along the side of the church, with views across to the Downs on your right. Take the smooth downhill run, fast or easy, into Ashington. At the junction with Meiro's Way, cycle **L**.

6 At the end of Rectory Lane, Cycle **L**.

NB: Or, if you're ready for a bite to eat, cycle **R** for about ¾km to find The Red Lion pub in Ashington which boasts family dining.

At the roundabout, take the second exit for a short cycle along the B2133 towards Billingshurst. Turn **R** up Spear Hill, continuing **SA** as it becomes Hooklands Lane. Pass Oxcopse Farm and Blonk's Farm on your left. Ignore the bridleway on your right.

7 Just beyond Blonk's Barn, turn **L** through a metal gate and ride along the bridleway. This track might be more idyllic on a summer's day, but on a wet day there are some great puddles to splash through.

When you reach a land boundary (currently wood and wire fence) go through the metal gate. Keep to the bridleway. Now that's easier said than done because it's not obvious where it runs but if you cycle **SA** and try to keep parallel with the edge of the trees, you should be okay. Watch out for the shy and nervous alpacas. Pass a wooden waymarker and follow the mud track to the gate. Follow the waymarked bridleway through a gate.

Before you cycle on, a word about the puddles: you might feel like you're diving waist-deep on your bike into a pond and since bikes don't float (well, not ours anyway) be ready to swim. On the other hand, you'll probably cycle this on a summer's day with the sun baking the earth under your wheels. In which case, the only thing to say is, good for you... Keep going. Pass a wooden waymarker.

Ride on through the farmyard and go through the gate onto the concrete bridleway.

8 At the B2133, cross **SA** onto Cray's Lane, passing the red letter box. Cycle back towards Thakeham. Pass Cray's Court on your right. Power or ponder your way up the hill in Thakeham, pausing by Thakeham Lodge if you wish. This might be a good moment to mention The White Lion free house, just up the road in the village...

downland views, forgotten forests & agricultural tracks

plumpton green // chiltington

route 6 // 14.5km (9 miles)

This route is excellent for those who enjoy cycling on a variety of bridleway surfaces. You will feel like you're exploring places where no bicycle has ever been before and you can admire the Downs in the distance without having to climb up any horrendously steep slopes.

There are two choices for the middle section of this route. We couldn't choose between them as they're both hugely enjoyable. Spin your tyres on leafy lanes or test your balance on off-road tracks – the choice is yours.

The climax of the route takes you through a fantastic wood through which you can cycle at whatever speed grabs your gears or suits your pedalling feet.

The ride starts in the centre of Plumpton Green. Look out for the village sign in black and gold, and signs for the Village Hall. Turn into West Gate and park by the side of the road.

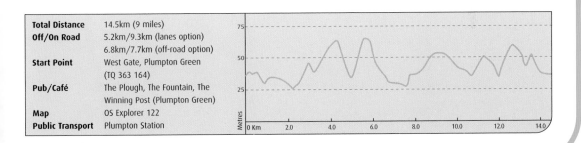

Total Distance	14.5km (9 miles)
Off/On Road	5.2km/9.3km (lanes option)
	6.8km/7.7km (off-road option)
Start Point	West Gate, Plumpton Green
	(TQ 363 164)
Pub/Café	The Plough, The Fountain, The
	Winning Post (Plumpton Green)
Map	OS Explorer 122
Public Transport	Plumpton Station

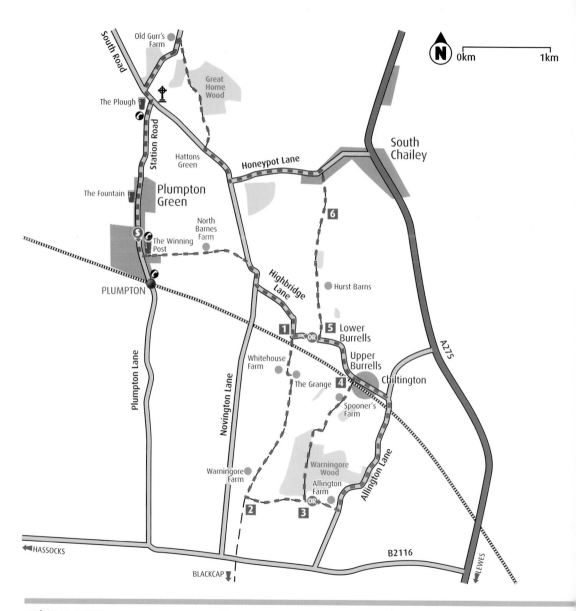

passing the white house and the blacksmiths. Stay on the lane. At the fork, see the post box opposite. Turn **R**. You are looking for the bridleway which you came down earlier. It is signed by a wooden post, just before the tiled house (Little Clears) on your left. Ride **L** up the concrete bridleway and turn **R** at The Winning Post pub.

Heading towards Hurst Barns Farm, you might want to build up some speed on this stony descent as there's an uphill to conquer on the other side, but do watch out for the big potholes and the speed bump at the bottom. At the top, turn back to check out those views to the Downs again. Cycle through the farm and look for a gate straight ahead in front of you at the top of the hill.

Unfortunately the bridleway here isn't well signed but you need to go **SA** through the gate next to the stile. The bridleway leads you down the grassy hill towards the gap in the hedge and up the field opposite. Go **SA** through the left-hand metal gate and onto the woodland bridleway. This track is likely to be challenging to keep your balance on. Whether dry and bone-shaking or sticky and muddy, we guarantee you'll be pleased to emerge onto the concrete bridleway.

6 Turn **R** and continue until you reach Honeypot Lane where you turn **L**. Upon reaching the T-junction, turn **R**. Ride down the lane, passing the cottages in Hattons Green on your right and look for a well-signed bridleway leading **R** into the trees just as you approach a slight slope. Soon you'll come to a wooden bridge (ignoring the bridge to the footpath which goes right). Continue **SA** on the bridleway across the bridge and cycle through Great Home Wood. This is one of our favourite woodland paths as it meanders through a forest-like haze of trees.

Take it at your own speed. It's worth noting that there are several small bridges ahead but they're relatively level. Emerge onto a mud track and follow the bridleway ahead. The track is narrow at points and there are nettles. The bridleway tips you out onto the road opposite Old Gurr's Farm. Turn **L** and pedal uphill and keep pedalling until you reach a T-junction. Turn **L** onto South Road towards Plumpton Green.

NB: Turn **R** for The Plough. Notice the Polish War Memorial.

Turn **R** on Station Road after The Plough and enjoy the downhill run back into Plumpton Green, past The Fountain.

out IN the sticks

BARNS GREEN // SLINFOLD

ROUTE 7 // 13.7km (8.5 miLes)

The beauty of this ride is that it brings you up close to agricultural Sussex without you ever having to do too much tough riding. Furthermore, given the route's proximity to Horsham and Southwater, there is a wonderful 'out in the sticks' feel to most sections.

There are one or two short hard climbs but most of the uphills are on tarmac surfaces. Any tougher sections of off-road riding are brief and balanced by the fact that the majority of the bridleways you'll cycle on are well-surfaced and pleasingly wide. What's more, there's a great downhill that gives the end of this ride an exhilarating finale!

You'll be using a section of the Downs Link Cycle Route that makes for easy riding. A long distance bridleway, the Downs Link runs along the bed of an old railway line and links between the North and South Downs.

The ride starts from the car parks near Barns Green recreation ground. Barns Green is between Horsham, Southwater and Billingshurst and the village is signed from most surrounding roads. Heading south on the Itchingfield-Billingshurst road (Plumtree Cross Lane) look out for the crossroads signed to Muntham House School in front of the village sign and football pitch. After turning right, the first hall on the right is Barns Green Village Club and the second is the village hall. Pick your parking with care as some is restricted.

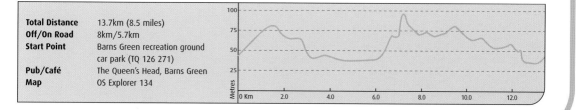

Total Distance	13.7km (8.5 miles)
Off/On Road	8km/5.7km
Start Point	Barns Green recreation ground car park (TQ 126 271)
Pub/Café	The Queen's Head, Barns Green
Map	OS Explorer 134

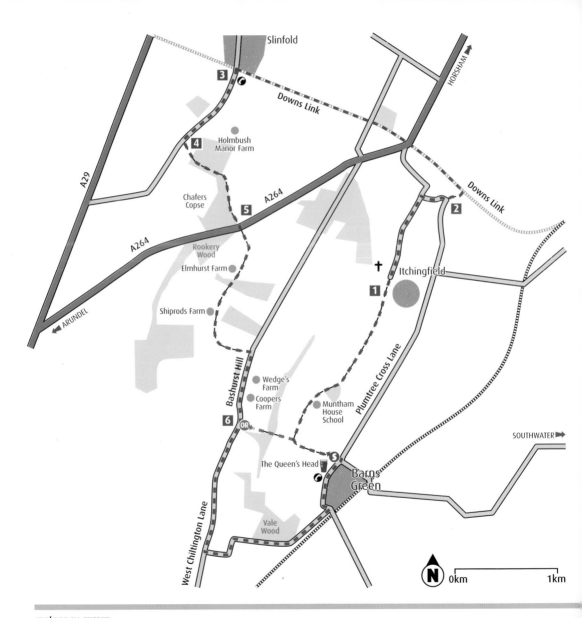

Slinfold

3

Downs Link

4

Holmbush
Manor Farm

HORSHAM

Downs Link

A29

Chafers
Copse

A264

5

2

A264

Rookery
Wood

Elmhurst Farm

✝ Itchingfield

1

Shiprods Farm

Bashurst Hill

Wedge's
Farm

Coopers
Farm

Muntham
House
School

Plumtree Cross Lane

ARUNDEL

SOUTHWATER ➤

6 OR

The Queen's Head

S

Barns
Green

West Chiltington Lane

Vale
Wood

N 0km 1km

Follow Trout Lane past the village hall and up a slight gradient. Pass the entrance to Muntham House School on your right. At the top of the hill, follow the lane as it curves round, ignoring the bridleway that forks off to your left. Cycle past Owlets House on your right. Pass through Muntham Home Farm, continuing **SA** on bridleway. You'll reach a wooden five-bar gate with imposing stone pillars, sculpted with rams' skulls. Go through this and follow the bridleway for approximately 1km.

1 You will reach a point where the bridleway joins a lane. Itchingfield Primary School sits on the corner. Cycle **SA** along the road. The views open out as you pedal. Upon arriving at a small T-junction, turn **R**.

2 Ride on, until just before a sharp bend in the road where you need to follow a **L** turn, signed Downs Link Bridleway. Pedal up the hill and across the brick bridge, over the old railway track that is now the Downs Link. On descending from the bridge, follow the green Downs Link sign that points **L**, doubling back on yourself. Pass a North Downs Way sign saying Slinfold 1½ miles. By the bridge, go **R** and cycle towards Slinfold. Notice an airstrip on your right. Pass under a brick bridge (the A264 runs above your head and we guess that's strangely preferable to it being under your wheels).

3 Reach a wooden gate and come out on a road of houses. Turn **L**. Pass Holmbush Manor on your left and enjoy a fairly easy run until you come to a horrible uphill. The good thing is that just when you reach the point where you hate both the hill and your bike, it's time to turn off.

4 After passing tile-fronted Hayes Hill Cottage, you'll see a wooden waymarked bridleway pointing **L**. Go through the gate and proceed diagonally south across the field towards Chafers Copse. Let's hope the name doesn't

Bike Hire

There's a good bike hire shop in Southwater: Southwater Cycles. If you want to join this route from the hire shop, you will need to cycle north on the Downs Link. This does include a short main road section. You will join our route at Instruction 2, the Downs Link section, by the bridge about 2½km from Slinfold. The most recognisable landmark is the airstrip.

Food & Drink

The Queen's Head in Barns Green is well-situated for a drink or more at the end of your ride. It's well-signed from the village crossroads. The baguettes are a meal in themselves and the stilton burger takes some beating.

Family Riding

Good surfaces, one off-road stretch that is tricky when wet, and ups and downs on country lanes, mean children need to be road-safe. It would suit older children on a dry day. Try the nearby shorter **Barns Green Mini-Circuit** on page 23 first.

prove to be prophetic. A chafer, by the way, is a large flying beetle with a tendency to be destructive.

Follow the wooden waymarked signs into the woods. This path is tougher when muddy. Follow the bridleway sign **R** at the edge of the woods and then continue to follow the edge of the woods down past the farm, keeping an eye out for large protruding tree roots. Cycle into Rookery Wood. If you dare, build some speed up down the hill towards the bridge to carry your bike up the short, steep slope on the other side. You'll end up at a gate, which leads onto the A264.

5 Cross, following the signed bridleway through the metal gate. Cycle along the gravelled bridleway between post and rail fences. Turn **R** at the end of the field following the bridleway track between Elmhurst Farm buildings. Go **SA** through the wooden gate and encourage your bike to follow the gentle contours of the track. If that fails, dismount and push. At the top, go through the metal gate.

Cycle **SA** towards the wooden gate. Ignore the first gate on the left to a private residence. Go through the wooden gate and follow this fantastic farmland bridleway. If your luck's in, a chorus of sheep will see you on your way. Come out at the entrance to Shiprods Farm. Turn **R** onto a metalled lane, passing Wedge's Farm and Coopers Farm.

6 **Optional Route:**
There's an off-road link back to the start here. It's not really a shortcut because it's probably tougher than the on-road route. If you don't mind a rather nasty off-road uphill, look out for the distinctive old red and brick timber house on your left. A signed bridleway precedes it. Go **L** down the bridleway and through a gate and up the other side to join back up with Trout Lane, turn **R** back to the Village Hall car park.

Alternatively, freewheel **SA** down Bashurst Hill. It turns into West Chiltington Lane. Resist Koi Carp World on your right if you can. Shortly before the red post box, you will see a white sign for Barns Green pointing left. Ride **L** down the whole length of Valewood Lane and a very enjoyable downhill it is too. The railway line runs alongside at one point but you hardly notice it. At a T-junction, turn **L** towards Barns Green. Pass the Hordens, Barns Green Stores and pass over the crossroads and back towards the car parks and Village Halls ahead.

UNDER WOLSTONBURY HILL

GODDARDS GREEN // HICKSTEAD // TWINEHAM // SAYERS COMMON

ROUTE 8 // 17.5 km (11 miles)

Whizz round quiet lanes, savour open agricultural views towards Wolstonbury Hill and the Downs, meander down idyllic bridleways and all without going up any hills. Well, almost...

This route has several possible diversions enabling you to do more on- or off-road cycling to suit both your preference and the wonderful British weather.

The starting point is the car park at The Sportsman in Goddards Green. This pub can be found south of the A2300 Hickstead to Burgess Hill road.

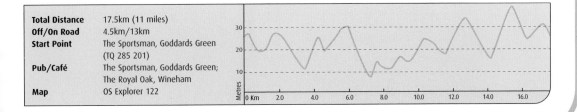

Total Distance	17.5km (11 miles)
Off/On Road	4.5km/13km
Start Point	The Sportsman, Goddards Green (TQ 285 201)
Pub/Café	The Sportsman, Goddards Green; The Royal Oak, Wineham
Map	OS Explorer 122

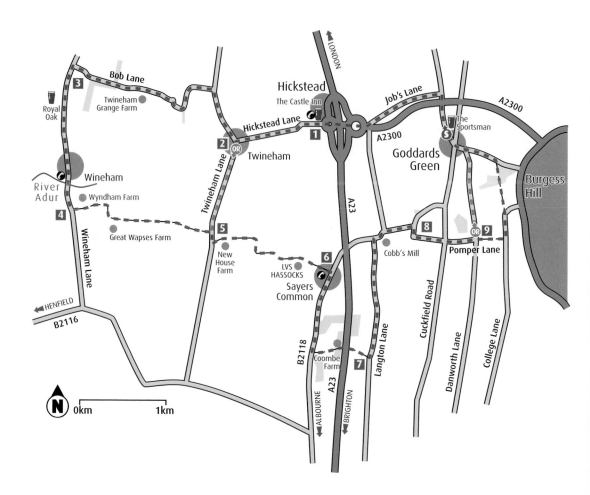

Royal
Oak

Bob Lane

3

Twineham
Grange Farm

Hickstead
The Castle Inn

Job's Lane

A2300

Hickstead Lane

1

The
Sportsman

2 OR

Twineham

A2300

5

Goddards
Green

Burgess
Hill

River
Adur

Wineham

Wyndham Farm

Wineham Lane

4

Great Wapses Farm

Twineham Lane

A23

5

New
House
Farm

LVS
HASSOCKS

6

8

Cobb's Mill

OR 9

Pomper Lane

Sayers
Common

Cuckfield Road

Danworth Lane

College Lane

HENFIELD

B2116

Langton Lane

B2118

Coombe
Farm

7

N

0km   1km

ALBOURNE

BRIGHTON

A23

LONDON

Turn **R** out of the pub car park and follow the blue cycle route towards Hickstead village. Cross over the A2300 – **be careful as it's a fast road**! Turn immediately **L** down Job's Lane, still following the signs for Hickstead Village. Cross one minor road, going **SA** until you reach the Hickstead roundabout with access to the A23.

The Crawley–Brighton cycle track runs beside the roundabout. Follow it **SA**, crossing the bridge over the A23. At the mini-roundabout on the other side, leave the cycle track, crossing to the left of The Castle Inn.

1 Your turn-off is Hickstead Lane, on the opposite side of the roundabout, signed Hickstead Village and Twineham. Cycle on.

2 As you approach Twineham, you reach a T-junction with a small war memorial. Go **R** along Chapel Road.

Optional Route:
This shortcut cuts about 1½km of off-road and about 3km of on-road cycling. Turn **L** along Twineham Lane through Twineham, over the bridge to rejoin the main route at Instruction 5.

After a red post box on your left, turn **L** into the singletrack road, Bob Lane. Ride for about 2½km, passing Twineham Grange Farm on your left.

3 At the next T-junction, turn **L** into Wineham Lane towards Wineham, passing the Royal Oak on your right. Continue past the traditional red phone box on your right, cross the bridge over the River Adur and look out for the gateway to the third property on your left, Wyndham Farm.

4 Turn **L**, following the bridleway through the gate and up the driveway towards Wyndham Farm. Pass through a

food & drink
The Sportsman is a friendly and comfortable real-ale pub that welcomes children, dogs, hikers and cyclists.

The picturesque **Royal Oak** near Wineham has a large garden and would make a good mid-route stop, A welcoming, traditional pub, the food is tasty and good value.

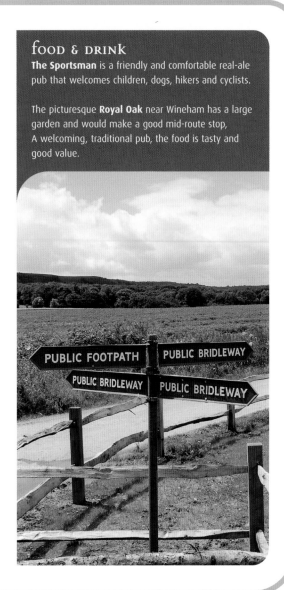

second gate and cross the farmyard. Head for the mud track which continues the bridleway **SA**. The first hundred metres or so can be muddy but it soon turns into a solid, clay path.

Pass through a metal farm gate and turn **R** onto a rough grassy bridleway. After a heavy downpour, it can become churned up as these fields are grazed by horses. At the wooden waymarker, turn **L** where the bridleway goes between the paddock fences. Continue through a metal gate, passing Great Wapses Farm on your right. Again, this bridleway is well used by horses and can become churned up if wet. Watch out for the white electric fence on your left. When you reach the next wooden gate, ride **SA** following the grassy path. Enjoy uplifting views stretching across grassy meadows towards distant Wolstonbury Hill. Bear left through some trees.

Let the easy-to-ride clay track lead you through the trees, ignoring a small concrete track that crosses your path. Keep going until you reach a metalled road.

5 Turn **R** into Twineham Lane (joining the shortcut from Instruction 2). Look out for first bridleway on your left at New House Farm. Cycle **L** along the bridleway, keeping an eye out for the Rehoming Centre for Retired Greyhounds on your left (visits by appointment only).

Just after the path slopes slightly downwards, you will reach a fork in front of a well-camouflaged pond. If you pass red-tiled Longhovel Cottage you have gone too far! Take the bridleway **R** before the pond.

At the bottom of the hill, where the concrete path curves to the right, take a sharp **L**, through the gate and across the field. There is no bridleway sign. Follow the track,

veering right towards a metal gate. Go through and follow the bridleway along the hedge towards the gate. Continue **SA** and you will emerge onto the driveway to LVS Hassocks.

6 Turn **R** into Sayers Common, taking care on this short section of main road (B2118). Ride **SA** at two small roundabouts. Ride **L** down the green-signed bridleway opposite a brick built bungalow (Coombe Down). Follow the concrete bridleway, keeping left at Coombe Farm and zip up over the bridge crossing the A23.

7 Turn **L** onto Langton Lane and coast down the gentle slope. Arrive at a T-junction opposite a thatched cottage and a red post box.

Turn **R** across a stone bridge. At Cobb's Mill Drive, if you feel the urge to stop, abandon your bikes for five minutes and take the public footpath across the garden and onto a wooden footbridge. This vantage point gives you a good view of the water mill working in all its glory. Grab your bikes and continue **SA**.

8 Just before the road bends left, turn **R** up Pomper Lane and see if you can spot Wolstonbury Hill (now seen from the other side). Cross Cuckfield Road, to continue along Pomper Lane.

Optional Route:
To avoid more off-road cycling, turn **L** into High Hatch Lane. This takes you all the way back to Gatehouse Lane. There's a slight slope to be tackled but it's good to know that the last stretch to the pub is pure downhill...

9 To continue an extra 1½km off-road, turn **R** into Danworth Lane and then **L** into a gated narrow bridleway. On a wet day, clay feels heavy underfoot but look on the bright side, the slope's going in the right direction and there are fantastic farmland views to your right. This clay path can become churned up but honestly, it does turn into a flatter, smoother mud track where the path goes through the trees.

Go through a gate and turn into College Lane. Come round a slight right-hand bend; notice the road slopes downward and look out for the concealed bridleway on the left beside a house with a five-bar gate. Take the bridleway, following the close-boarded fence on your left.

At the end of the bridleway, turn **L** into Gatehouse Lane and cycle the last kilometre or so back to The Sportsman!

folklore wolstonbury hill

King Alfred is said to have fought on Wolstonbury Hill and the ten horseshoes that are on the Bull Hotel at Ditchling are said to have been cast by his ponies. Watch out. According to an old rhyme,

**"When Wolstonbury has a cap
Hurstpierpoint will get a drap."**

In other words, if Wolstonbury Hill is covered by cloud, pedal fast. Rain will follow at Hurstpierpoint but at least you're heading in the other direction.

out of sight near ditchling

ditchling // wivelsfield // streat

route 9 // 12.9km (8 miles)

This trail starts a short ride away from Ditchling, a picturesque village which boasts both an interesting history and some superb eating places. The only through roads can become very busy, so we've located our quiet circular route just up the road where you'll discover some of the almost untouched backwaters of Sussex.

All lanes selected for this route are quiet. The off-road cycling is rewarding, both in terms of downland vistas and because there's a couple of woodland bridleways where you'll be doing well to keep your balance without putting your feet down. Never mind, there's nothing wrong with getting off and pushing your bike...

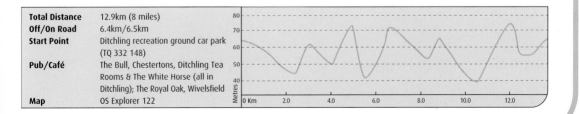

Total Distance	12.9km (8 miles)	
Off/On Road	6.4km/6.5km	
Start Point	Ditchling recreation ground car park (TQ 332 148)	
Pub/Café	The Bull, Chestertons, Ditchling Tea Rooms & The White Horse (all in Ditchling); The Royal Oak, Wivelsfield	
Map	OS Explorer 122	

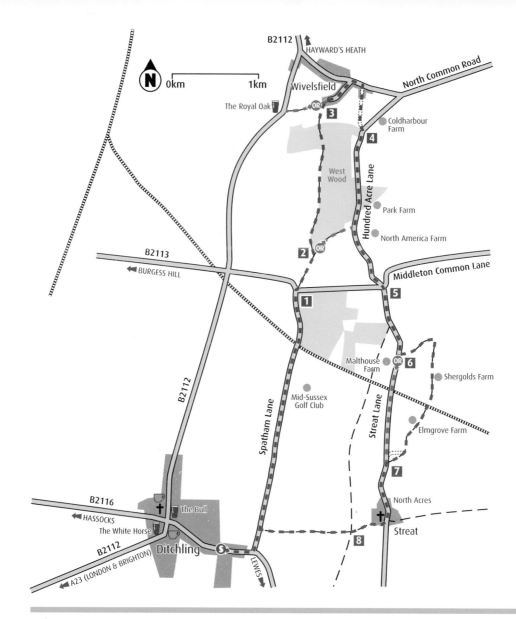

B2112
HAYWARD'S HEATH

North Common Road

Wivelsfield

The Royal Oak

OR **3**

Coldharbour
Farm

4

West
Wood

Hundred Acre Lane

Park Farm

North America Farm

B2113
BURGESS HILL

2 OR

Middleton Common Lane

1

5

B2112

Spatham Lane

Mid-Sussex
Golf Club

Malthouse
Farm OR **6**

Shergolds Farm

Streat Lane

Elmgrove Farm

7

North Acres

B2116
HASSOCKS
The Bull
The White Horse

B2112
A23 (LONDON & BRIGHTON)

Ditchling

S

LEWES

Streat

8

0km 1km

N

Start from the car park attached to Ditchling Recreation Ground. Head east from Ditchling on the B2116 towards Westmeston/Lewes and you'll find it on the left.

Turn **L** out of the car park and after a short distance, turn **L** into Spatham Lane. Cycle along Spatham Lane, past the golf course and up the hill over the railway line.

1 Reach a fork, where you take a **R** towards Plumpton. Immediately **L**, there's a green bridleway signed to Wivelsfield Green. After you cycle past some cottages, the gravelled bridleway narrows and goes through a wood (long trousers advised for those who like protection from brambles and nettles).

2 At the fork, turn **L**.

Optional Route:

Turn **R** at the fork to shorten the route by approximately 3 km and avoid the off-road section through West Wood. You'll rejoin the main route just after Instruction 4.

You are riding into West Wood. This woodland bridleway is great fun to ride but the mud track can be bumpy and you need to watch out for roots and debris! If you keep the barbed wire fence roughly on your left, you can't lose the path. Can you ride through the whole wood without putting your feet down?

You'll ride over two small wooden bridges. The approach to the second bridge, which runs over a small stream, can be very muddy. Continue until you begin to emerge from the wood where you follow the track keeping Woods Cottage on your right. Soon you'll reach Eastern Road in Wivelsfield.

family RIDING

The advantage of this circuit is that it includes a number of options so that you can tailor your route to the needs of your party, splitting into two groups if you wish. Families with young children could consider the church at Streat (Instruction 7) as an alternative starting point to avoid the short section along the B2116.

food & DRINK

If you wish to ride on into Ditchling, prepare yourself for the traffic calming measures and look out for the following eating places.

The Bull – a popular pub with a grassy garden and the food goes down a treat.

Chestertons – with a hideaway walled courtyard and coffee and goodies to die for.

Ditchling Tea Rooms – a popular teashop. The garage beside the café is available for cyclists to park their bikes in.

The White Horse – a traditional pub with good food. Chilli, chips and cheese are a favourite plus well-kept Harveys and a courtyard garden.

Or watch out for **The Royal Oak**, a short way into the ride: a pleasant free house with a good garden for children.

NB: At Eastern Road, turn **L** and follow the jungle tracks through ferns and Ditchling Common Country Park to emerge opposite The Royal Oak on the B2112. This is a free house with a good garden for children.

3 Turn **R** at Eastern Road and cycle until you reach a T-junction. Cycle a short distance **R** along North Common Road. A pavement runs beside the road. Keep an eye out for a bridleway on your **R** marked by a ground-level stone marker next to Field House. Follow the track, watching out for mud and roots! Cross a small bar and gate bridge and take a deep breath before tackling the short uphill stretch **SA**. There's no shame in pushing if you prefer. Before you know it you'll be coming out at Hundred Acre Lane opposite Cold Harbour Nursery.

4 Turn **R** and the uphill will seem much easier now you're on the road. Soon, you can enjoy the smooth downhill descent. West Wood is now on your right and you pass Park Farm and North America Farm on your left.

(The Optional Route from Instruction 2 now merges with the main route.)

Cycle **L** at the T-junction with Middleton Common Lane.

5 As you quickly approach a bend in Middleton Common Lane, be ready to turn **R** onto Streat Lane. Be careful because you have to turn on an uphill gradient and your vision is restricted by the bend! Coast down Streat Lane. Ignore Kents Lane bridleway to Westmeston and continue **SA**.

6 Where the road curves down a hill and the view opens onto the Downs ahead, look out for signs for Hortons and Deans Farm on your left. If you pass Malthouse Farm on your right, you've gone too far.

Take this track left, continuing on the bridleway and bear right until you reach the end of the grey gravelled path in front of a red brick double-fronted house. Follow the bridleway **R** cycling between wide converging hedges that enable you to enjoy the views as you approach the Downs. Can you spot a V-shaped group of trees up on the South Downs? More about this later...

Come to a metal gate and go through **SA**. This is a fantastic downhill stretch on rough grass with fine views towards the Downs. Pass Shergolds Farm and continue **SA** through a five-bar gate and enjoy the rest of this grassy run downhill.

Go through another metal gate and across a wooden bridge, where the sounds of the water might make you pause. Watch out for bricks in the mud track ahead and the step up to the small wooden bridge that crosses under the railway tunnel. From time to time, trains on the Haywards Heath to Lewes line pass overhead.

A short muddy narrow section through nettles comes next but the bridleway opens out as you reach an open field. Continue **SA** on the track across the rough meadow, keeping Elmgrove Farm on your right. The bridleway goes through some trees and reaches a metal gate. Continue, following the track into the woods. Pass a five-bar gate on your left just before the track curves right to where a metal gate is dwarfed by hedges. Go through this and turn **R**, continuing around and down the side of the field to where a gap beside a gate leads directly back onto Streat Lane.

Optional Route:

To avoid more off-road, at the start of 6 instead continue straight down Streat Lane, enjoying the easy downhill run, rejoining the main route at Instruction 7. The hedged lanes can be quite narrow so keep to the sides.

7 Turn **L** (merging with optional route here). Ride up the slope past North Acres B&B. At the top of the hill, go past a post box and then take the footpath leading **R** in front of the telephone box and Streat Church. **Please dismount and push your bike down this short section of wide footpath**, watching out for stones.

To your left, take a closer look at the V-shaped group of trees planted on the South Downs above Streat to commemorate the Silver Jubilee of Queen Victoria. An 'R' was also planned but they ran out of money before it was finished.

8 The footpath emerges at Hayleigh Farm. Turn **L** and then **R** along this well-signed bridleway running along the foot of the Downs. When you reach Spatham Lane, turn **L** and then **R** onto the B2116. You will see the recreation ground car park on your right.

OUT OF SIGHT NEAR DITCHLING

RIVER ADUR, PEACEFUL GLADES AND DOWNS LINK

HENFIELD // PARTRIDGE GREEN // ASHURST

ROUTE 10 // 17.7km (11 MILES)

Discover wooded glades and farmland landscapes. This route combines stretches of the Downs Link with peaceful lanes and off-road bridleways. There are one or two uphill climbs but the most demanding cycling takes place off-road. The extra effort is well worth it to gain the peaceful ambience, glimpses of wildlife and views along the River Adur. Take time to stop at twelfth century St James Church if you are so inclined...

Start in Henfield at the car park by the Downs Link. The A281 runs through Henfield. Turn off westwards into Church Street and continue into Upper Station Road. You cannot miss the car park that is just beyond The Old Railway Tavern.

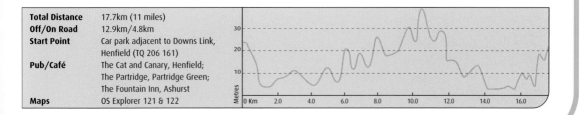

Total Distance	17.7km (11 miles)
Off/On Road	12.9km/4.8km
Start Point	Car park adjacent to Downs Link, Henfield (TQ 206 161)
Pub/Café	The Cat and Canary, Henfield; The Partridge, Partridge Green; The Fountain Inn, Ashurst
Maps	OS Explorer 121 & 122

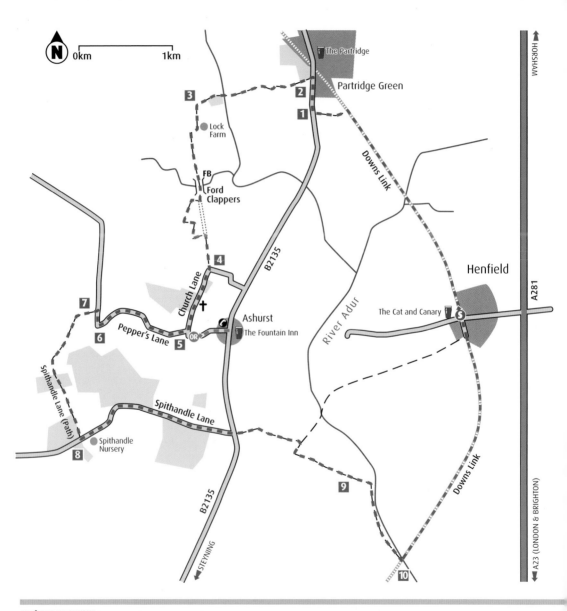

N 0km 1km

The Partridge

Partridge Green

Lock Farm

Downs Link

3

2

1

FB
Ford
Clappers

B2135

Henfield

River Adur

The Cat and Canary

4

Church Lane

Ashurst
The Fountain Inn

7

6

Pepper's Lane

5
OR

Spithandle Lane (path)

Spithandle Lane

Spithandle Nursery

8

9

B2135

STEYNING

Downs Link

10

Go through the gap beside the metal gate and ride north on the Downs Link for just over 2km. Pass through the wooden gate and follow the grassy left-hand track. On the other side of the field, go through another wooden gate and follow the compacted stone bridleway **L** to Partridge Green.

1 Turn **R** at the road. There's a very short stretch of the B2135 here. For most of this, children can push their bikes on the pavement.

NB: Down to earth, friendly pub, The Partridge is over the bridge and on the right.

2 Where the B2135 starts to go uphill and before you reach the bridge, break away from the Downs Link by taking a **L** into the bridleway, signed Lock Estate Private Road. Occasional vehicles access the farms and houses along this road.

The bridleway crosses the river and starts to go uphill, curving to the left. Pass Lock House on your right and almost immediately look left for the entrance to Lock Farm. Take the grassy bridleway that runs alongside the hedge, parallel to the metalled road that you have been following.

3 Towards the top of the hill, the track veers sharply **L** through a farm and some houses. At the T-junction where Quince Cottage stands on the corner, turn **L** and continue along the bridleway.

Watch out for the concrete step up to the wooden bridge at Ford Clappers! (Deirdre should know. Testing the route in the opposite direction, she came a cropper at Ford Clappers, impaling herself in ungraceful fashion on the bridge, narrowly avoiding a nettle bath.)

LOCAL KNOWLEDGE
The simple but beautiful parish church of St James in Ashurst is well worth exploring. The earliest part of the building dates from the 12th Century. In the north-east area of the churchyard, close to the eastern boundary, is an oak cross set in a stone base to Margeret Fairless Dawson who died 24 August 1901, aged 33. Mrs Dawson, who used the nom de plume Michael Fairless, was the author of **The Roadmender** (1902), which was set in the Ashurst area. Look and see what words are inscribed on the horizontal arm of the cross.

family RIDING
There are no shortcuts on our circuit here so only take children that you are confident can cope with the length of the route and the off-road sections.

Cross the bridge and follow the bridleway. The grassy path goes uphill and, especially when muddy, it can be difficult to make the gradient without dismounting. At the top of the hill, the path winds down with views across fields on your right. Look out for the animals when you pass through the farmyard and workshops. Beyond the farmyard, turn **R** keeping to the public bridleway.

4 At the T-junction by Holly Lodge turn **R** into metalled Church Lane, looking out for St James Church on your left.

5 At the black and white stripy signpost, join Pepper's Lane cycling **R** in the direction of Dial Post. Traffic is occasional but can be fast.

NB: Alternatively, turn **L** joining School Lane in the direction of Partridge Green. Ride past the school and when you reach the nearby T-junction with the B2135, you can see The Fountain Inn to your left. Note that children under ten are not allowed inside this 16th Century pub due to uneven floorboards (health and safety?!) but there is a pleasant garden.

6 Back on Pepper's Lane keep right at the post box where the road bends. A short distance later, turn **L** at the wooden bridleway marker and sign marked Jessops. Ride on.

7 Where the road veers left, look out for a metal gate on your left and a wooden waymarker leading into fields. Follow the bridleway **L** through two fields and along a wide grassy avenue between two hedges. This section can be muddy. Beyond the third (and muddiest) gate, join Spithandle Pathway and continue on the well-maintained bridleway, soaking up the woodland atmosphere... The ride through the copse has an idyllic feel and is well worth the trip across the fields.

8 Go through a metal gate and turn **L** onto Spithandle Lane. Plant-lovers may want to look out for Spithandle Nursery on the right. Enjoy the pleasant downward run, keeping an eye out for deer. You will reach the B2135. Cross with care, following the bridleway directly opposite. Where the bridleway forks in front of a house, do not go straight on but **keep R** along the metalled road. Follow the farm track around to the left. Savour the downland views and soon you'll reach a metal gate.

9 At the gate, the bridleway continues into the field ahead. Any cows present should be treated with respect! On the banks of the River Adur, turn **R**, following the grassy bridleway that runs alongside the river. Pass through four gates and rejoin the Downs Link.

10 Go **L** across the bridge and follow the pleasant Downs Link trail. When it ends, turn **R** into Holland Lane then **L** into Lower Station Road, up the short hill and **L** back towards the car park.

NB: Drop in at The Cat and Canary. It is open all day.

a forest, two fords and some fishing ponds

horsted keynes

route 11 // 12.9km (8 miles)

This route is good for those who like a smooth ride. Park your car in Horsted Keynes, a charming village with a mention in the Doomsday Book and follow a beautiful section of the Mid-Sussex Border Path from which you can admire a variety of fishing ponds. Climb through the Ashdown Forest on the quietest lanes that we could find before resting at Warren Peace Viewpoint. Finish off with a pedal-spinning downhill run and a forest track.

It's true that the route does involve a fair bit of up and down but the hills don't feel too arduous because the surfaces are good, the rural scenery's uplifting and you can't help but feel like you are miles from anywhere. Oh yes – and as if that isn't enough, there are a couple of fords you can splash through if you feel so inclined.

In Horsted Keynes, there's a well-signed free car park along Chapel Lane beside the Royal British Legion. This is your start point.

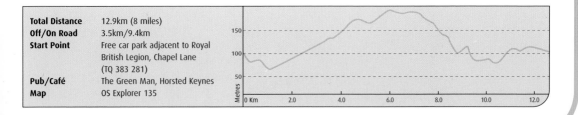

Total Distance	12.9km (8 miles)
Off/On Road	3.5km/9.4km
Start Point	Free car park adjacent to Royal British Legion, Chapel Lane (TQ 383 281)
Pub/Café	The Green Man, Horsted Keynes
Map	OS Explorer 135

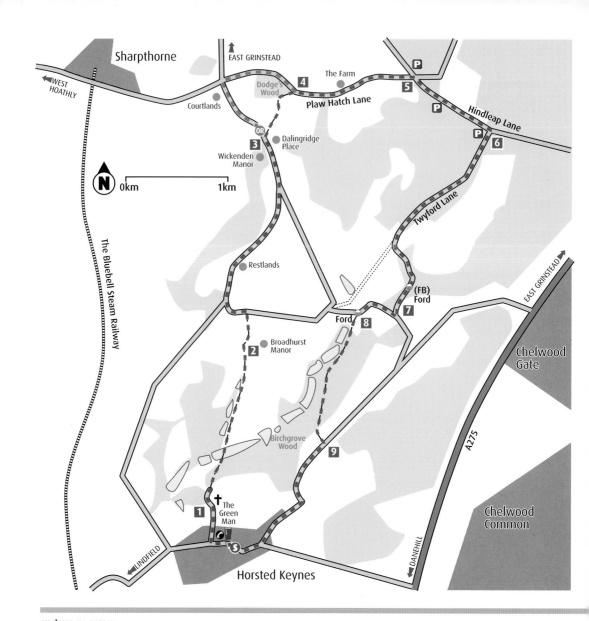

Sharpthorne

WEST HOATHLY

EAST GRINSTEAD

Courtlands

Dodge's Wood

4

The Farm

Plaw Hatch Lane

5

Hindleap Lane

OR
3

Dalingridge Place

Wickenden Manor

6

N
0km   1km

Twyford Lane

Restlands

(FB) Ford

The Bluebell Steam Railway

Ford

7

8

Broadhurst Manor

2

EAST GRINSTEAD

Chelwood Gate

Birchgrove Wood

9

A275

1

† The Green Man

Chelwood Common

LINDFIELD

S

DANEHILL

Horsted Keynes

Leave the car park past the British Legion. Cross the road and go between the concrete bollards and take the short ride down to Church Lane. Turn **R** and follow Church Lane **down** the hill.

1 You'll pass St Giles church at the top of the hill. Keep going. You are now on the West Sussex Border Path. Pass through the gap in the gate and continue **SA**. The path is bordered on both sides by a number of peaceful fishing ponds. Various angling clubs own the rights but there are plenty of benches and it's a wonderful spot to spend five minutes reflecting upon the world. Back on course, keep your eyes peeled for waterfalls as you follow the West Sussex Border Path **SA**.

2 Look out for the entrance and boundaries of **Animaline** in the grounds of Broadhurst Manor. Go through the gate and turn **L** up the slope. At the top, ride **L** and cycle until you reach the T-junction. Turn **R** towards Forest Row and cycle up the lane. There's a great feeling of space to be had as vistas of Sussex farmland open out through the hedgerows. Pass Restlands Farm on your right.

Keep going up this slow, thigh-burning hill. Pass the entrance to Wickenden Manor at the top. Look out for a large white house on the left that is partially masked by trees. Roughly opposite the house is a leafy bridleway leading off to the right. It has a difficult to spot wooden waymarker. If you reach Wickenden Manor Staff Entrance, you've gone too far.

3 To stay off-road, go **R** up the short, steep bridleway. Cross a driveway, and hurry past the 'stork' statue on the gatepost if it makes you feel nervous. This is Dalingridge Place. Follow the sign to the cottages but ignore the wooden gate, bearing left up the bridleway through

Dodge's Wood. Sections of this bridleway could be muddy in wet weather.

Emerge from Dodge's Wood onto a tarmac driveway and follow it to the right. Continue until you reach Plaw Hatch Lane. Go **R** up the slope.

Optional Route:

To take the on-road route, don't turn **R** onto the short, steep bridleway but instead go down the hill to the triangular junction. Courtlands Nursery is on the left and offers teas and plants for sale. Turn **R** onto the sometimes busy Plaw Hatch Lane and power up the hill, rejoining the main route.

4 Pass Plaw Hatch Farm Shop on your left. This organic farm shop is well worth a wander – even if just to savour the aroma of freshly baked bread and the sweet tang of fruit. Be warned though, there are some tempting snacks on offer. Continue up the slope, consoling yourself with the thought that what goes up must come down.

5 Arrive at a crossroads and turn **R** along Hindleap Lane, following the sign towards Wych Cross. You are now cycling through the edge of the Ashdown Forest (if you want an alternative start point for this route, there are numerous car parks in this area). The first car park on your right, marked with a wooden sign saying Hindleap, provides a good place to stop for five minutes. There's an information panel and Warren Peace Viewpoint looks out over Ashdown Forest. Cycle along the road until you see a white sign for Twyford.

6 Turn **R** down Twyford Lane, passing Twyford car park on your right. You can now indulge yourself with a fantastically long downhill descent through Ashdown Forest. Let your tyres spin... At the bottom of the hill,

look out for a ford, splashing through it with pizzazz. Some people might want to go through the ford more than once whilst others may prefer to use the footbridge. Suit your fancy. Follow the lane as it curves round and up. Trees stretch skyward from the bank above you

7 Upon reaching a staggered crossroads, turn sharp **R**. Enjoy the downhill but do watch out for potholes. On turning a bend towards the base of the hill, you'll see another ford ahead. The next bridleway is on your left, beside a gate and before you reach the ford. Before riding on, you may want to feel water under your wheels. Feel free to investigate the ford.

8 Turn **L** onto the bridleway before the ford and follow the dirt track through Birchgrove Wood. Mud abounds at the start when wet so look for the grassy edges. You'll see a fishing pond down to your right. In dry, sunny weather the track becomes sandy giving the path a continental feel. In season, watch out for grouse crossing the track but even **more importantly**, make sure you take the left fork because the right one is signposted FIREARMS IN USE.

Try to keep a steady pace on the uphill but push if you want to. Emerge from the woods bearing left onto a track between two fields. Head for the rickety gate leading onto the road.

9 Turn **R** and head straight back along the road into the centre of Horsted Keynes where your car park will be easy to spot. You may feel the pull of the pub... try The Green Man, on the village green. It's said to be built on the site of the old workhouse.

ifield conservation village, country lanes & green fields

faygate // ifield // rusper

route 12 // 16.1km (10 miles)

This route has the advantage of being close to two stations: Faygate at the start and Ifield close to the Optional Route. It is possible to ride this route in wet weather, especially if you pick the on-road option at the end. There's a small amount of off-road – enough to make you feel you're out in the countryside but nothing too arduous. It's surprising how quickly you can reach agricultural countryside when cycling from a large town such as Crawley.

The roads are busier in this area but we've tried hard to find the quietest lanes and the Optional Route should help you choose what suits you best. The main route goes past Ifield Mill and the Optional Route leads you on through Ifield Village Conservation Area and The Plough Inn. If you don't like cycling in traffic, you may wish to consider re-tracing your footsteps from the pub rather than continuing on the

Optional Route. We're assuming that it's the pub you're diverting towards; it could equally be the plaque to Elizabeth Fry on the house next door. There are several climbs but you're rewarded with fine, open views over fields and the resulting downhills give you the chance to draw breath. Any climbs are on smooth road surfaces and are not too long.

Your start point is Faygate Station so why not travel by public transport? If you come by car, follow signs for Faygate from the dual carriageway (A264) and park either in the car park of the Holmbush Inn or, if it's the weekend and you intend to take refreshment elsewhere, you shouldn't have a problem finding a suitable roadside spot. This route enables you to pedal right out into the tranquillity of the countryside from the cycle network within Crawley. Cyclists coming from Crawley may wish to join the route at Point 4. Ifield Station is also easily accessible from this point.

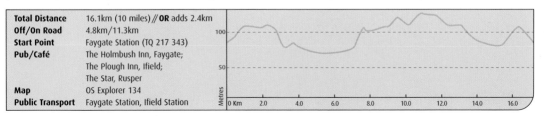

Total Distance	16.1km (10 miles) // **OR** adds 2.4km
Off/On Road	4.8km/11.3km
Start Point	Faygate Station (TQ 217 343)
Pub/Café	The Holmbush Inn, Faygate; The Plough Inn, Ifield; The Star, Rusper
Map	OS Explorer 134
Public Transport	Faygate Station, Ifield Station

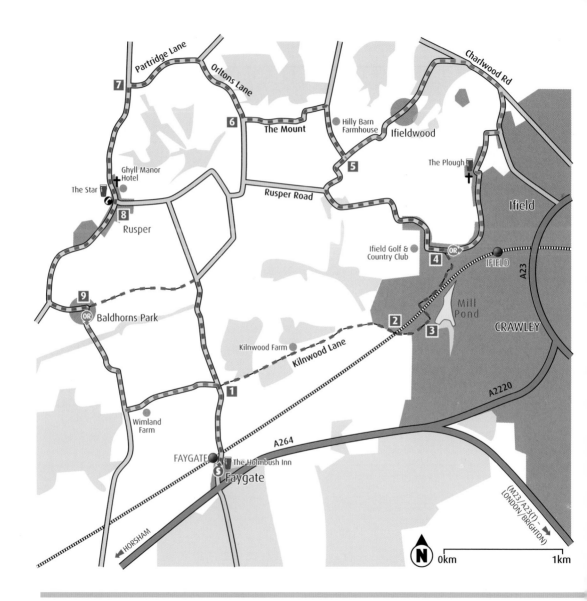

Partridge Lane

Orltons Lane

7

6

The Mount

Hilly Barn
Farmhouse

Ifieldwood

Charlwood Rd

The Plough

Ghyll Manor
Hotel

The Star

5

Ifield

8

Rusper

Rusper Road

Ifield Golf &
Country Club

OR **4**

IFIELD

A23

Mill
Pond

CRAWLEY

9

OR Baldhorns Park

2

3

Kilnwood Farm

Kilnwood Lane

A2220

1

Wimland
Farm

FAYGATE The Holmbush Inn

S Faygate

A264

HORSHAM

(M23/A23(T) –
LONDON/BRIGHTON)

N

0km   1km

Turn **L** out of the station or pub car park. Pedal hard to make the steady climb up the lane.

1 At the top, turn **R** along Kilnwood Lane. Cycle along the lane, passing Kilnwood Farm and Kilnwood Bungalow. By the sprawling house called Kilnwood End, the track narrows. Follow the bridleway **SA**, passing the pond on your left. Follow the bridleway **SA** through the woods. Note houses on your left. Continue **SA**. Enjoy the gradual downhill on this bridleway, keeping an eye out for roots.

2 At the wooden waymarker, turn **R**. Go through the metal gate and take care crossing the railway tracks. Continue a short distance.

3 At the next wooden waymarker, turn **L**. You emerge on the edge of a housing estate with Ifield Mill Pond to your right. Continue **SA**. At the end of St Francis Walk, cross the road (Waterfield Gardens) and before Collins Road, cycle **L** along the path that goes over the railway bridge. After the bridge, cycle **R**, following bridleway signs. Ride on until you reach Ifield Mill and the weir. Follow the path around to the yellow height barrier. For those who don't know the area, this off-road bridleway leads you onto a 'town' road; watch out for the traffic. Cycle **R** along Hyde Drive.

4 At the roundabout, ride **L** along Rusper Road. Carry on past Ifield Golf and Country Club. Cycle for some distance out into the countryside. The road narrows and you cross a small stone bridge over a stream. You are now approaching a tricky turn. There's a blind bend left and you must turn **R** into Ifieldwood. Cycle on.

At the roundabout, cycle **R** along Ifield Drive to take the Optional Route through Ifield Conservation Village and The Plough Inn. This OR does involve cycling on town roads. The stretch along Charlwood Road is particularly busy and we personally prefer to retrace our tyre tracks from the pub back to the main route, but the circular option is included for traffic-hardened cyclists.

Cycle on past Rusper Road playing fields. Turn **L** into Ifield Street and Ifield Village Conservation Area. Continue to The Plough Inn where you may wish to eat, drink or at the very least, check out the house next door. From the pub, cycle **L** down Rectory Lane and continue **R** before Tweed Lane. At the end of Rectory Lane, go **L** along Ifield Green. At the T-junction, turn **L** onto Charlwood Road, and the kind of fast-moving traffic that cyclists wear hi-visibility vests for. Turn **L** into the quieter Ifieldwood and follow the road to rejoin the main route at Instruction 5.

5 The two routes join together at the black and white signpost where you turn into Hillybarn Road. The name may make the long steady hill less of a surprise but unfortunately, it doesn't make it any the less painful. Pass Hilly Barn Farmhouse and begin to descend. Soon turn **L** into The Mount.

6 At the junction, cycle **R** along Orltons Lane. Don't fall off your bike when a plane passes overhead as you climb the hill – you're right under a Gatwick Airport flight path. At the top, turn **L** following the sign for Newdigate and cycle on until you reach the end of Partridge Lane. This is a very enjoyable downhill on a good gradient; steep enough to minimise effort without having to worry about going too fast. Here, the lane joins with Rusper Road.

7 Cycle **L**. Ride along what turns into Newdigate Road. It's a slow, steady climb. Cycle on into Rusper past Ghyll Manor Hotel and The Plough, and Attic Rooms, which allows smart dress only. If you wish to stop, The Star is not far...

8 At the junction in front of The Star, cycle **R**. After a gentle downhill run, cycle some way. Turn **L** towards Faygate at the red post box.

9 Where the road curves to the right, you can make a choice. To continue off-road on the main route cycle **SA**, following the bridleway into Baldhorns Park. Ride **SA** past the first wooden waymarker opposite the gate, ignoring the footpath leading left across the bridge. Ride along the bridleway until you reach a fork by a second pond. Do not cross the bridge. Follow the wooden waymarker along the **R** fork. Go through a wooden gate.

By the metal gate at the end of the field, cycle **L**. Ride over the stream and between two wooden fences. Go **R** through the wooden gate, following the bridleway sign. Ride **SA** across the field. Head through the right-hand gate and follow the bridleway signs **SA**. Follow the wooden waymarked bridleway diagonally right towards the small wooden bridge. Ride over the bridge and continue on. Cycle along this mud track. It will narrow and eventually merges with a tarmac driveway. Keep going, following the wooden-signed bridleway. Emerge onto the Faygate Road. Turn **R** and cycle up the hill. See if you can make it to the top... Pass Carylls Lodge. Keep **SA**, up the hill and back down to your Faygate starting point.

Optional Route:

To stay on-road, continue **R** on the road and up Wimland Road. Turn **L** at the white signpost into Wimland Lane. Pass Wimland Farm on your right. At the crossroads, turn **R** down the hill and back to Faygate.

OLDLAND MILL
CIRCA 1703

BeNeath the DOWNS

HassOcks // DitchLing // Burgess HiLL

ROUte 13 // 17.7km (11 miLes)

There's almost too much to take in on this ride. Skirt round Hurstpierpoint on stunning lanes, passing historic Danny House to follow the base of the Downs from Wolstonbury Hill to Ditchling Beacon Nature Reserve. The views towards this Area of Outstanding Natural Beauty are both imposing and stunning. Nip back through the woods and pedal along the back roads of interesting Ditchling before heading up to Oldland Mill. Finish off with a satisfying loop to Burgess Hill.

There are several uphills on this route but most are not too long and all are doable. It's just that you might not choose to do them all on the same day... pushing your bike is perfectly acceptable. The bridleways vary from narrow to wide, muddy to concrete. They'll take you through a golf course and past a variety of houses. The trickier sections are fairly short and well spread out. There are also one or two unavoidable stretches of road with more traffic than we'd ideally like.

The ride starts from The Friars Oak pub, on the A273 in Hassocks. This friendly and comfortable pub hides a lurid history of smuggling that can only be guessed at. If you use the car park, please let the landlords know that you'll be popping in for a drink and/or food after your ride.

An alternative start point is Hassocks station for those of you who prefer public transport. Emerge on the west side (Platform 1) and cycle **SA**. Turn **R** into Stanford Avenue. Towards the end of Stanford Avenue, take the third turning **R** into Stonepound Road. This is part of the Brighton to Burgess Hill cycleway but the signs are facing the other way. At the crossroads, go **SA** into Priory Road, following the blue cycle route signs. Turn **L**, still following the blue cycle route. At the T-junction, turn **R** to use a short stretch of the cycle path that runs alongside the busy A273. Join the start of the route at The Friars Oak.

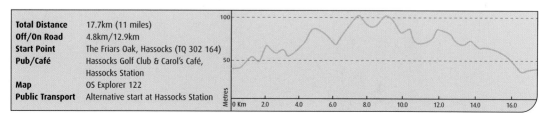

Total Distance	17.7km (11 miles)	
Off/On Road	4.8km/12.9km	
Start Point	The Friars Oak, Hassocks (TQ 302 164)	
Pub/Café	Hassocks Golf Club & Carol's Café, Hassocks Station	
Map	OS Explorer 122	
Public Transport	Alternative start at Hassocks Station	

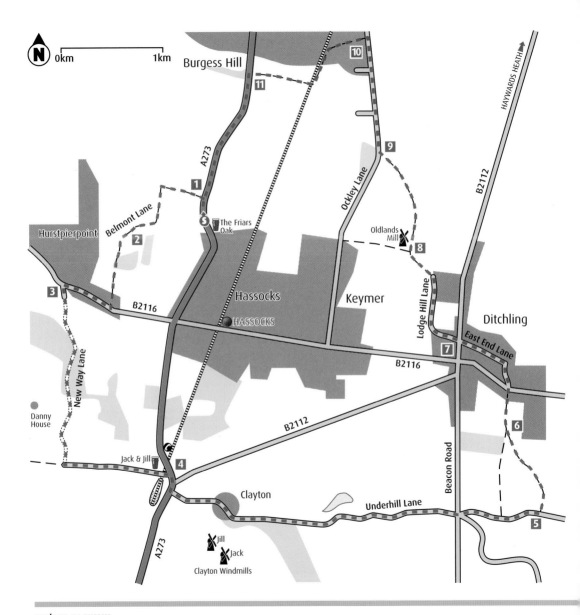

N 0km 1km

Burgess Hill

A273

Belmont Lane

Hurstpierpoint

The Friars Oak

Hassocks

HASSOCKS

Keymer

Ockley Lane

Oldlands Mill

Lodge Hill Lane

Ditchling

East End Lane

B2112

HAYWARDS HEATH

B2116

New Way Lane

Danny House

B2112

Jack & Jill

Clayton

Underhill Lane

Beacon Road

A273

Jill

Jack

Clayton Windmills

Turn **R** from The Friars Oak, following the blue cycle signs and riding a short section of the cycle path which runs alongside the busy A273.

1 Turn **L** where you see the white Friars Oak House sign, crossing the road and following the bridleway through the golf course. Continue to the end. Turn **L** and keep following the bridleway. Keep your eyes peeled; we saw a grass snake along this path once. The bridleway becomes a tarmac surface. Continue **SA**.

2 At a junction of bridleways turn **R**. You are now cycling on leafy Belmont Lane. Watch out for the speed bumps as you follow it around and down (oh, and up again). Turn **R** onto the busy road and take care on the downhill. As you approach the bend in the road, be ready to turn **L** into New Way Lane (it's hidden from view until the last moment).

3 Turn **R** onto the singletrack road. Pass the private drive to Danny House on your right. Continue **SA**. This lane is very quiet but it's worth remembering that cars are allowed on it too. There's a good view of imposing Danny House and the equally imposing Wolstonbury Hill. Take your pick. The lane bears round to the left. Notice the bridleway up to Wolstonbury Hill on your right. Come back another day and try it if you dare. Our route continues.

Make the most of the next down; the up takes some beating. Those who want to tackle Wolstonbury next can look on this slope as a starter hill... Catch your breath at the top and admire the views to the windmills on your right and across fields on your left. Cycle on.

4 Next to the Jack and Jill pub, turn **R** onto a very short section of the A273. Take the second road on the **L** into Underhill Lane signed Clayton. Follow this lane along the

Local knowledge
Elizabethan **Danny House** may be a retirement home now but on 13th October 1918, something important took place here. Prime minister Lloyd George met with his wartime cabinet and they agreed the terms of the Armistice to be offered to Germany at the end of the Great War.

family riding
This route is fine for older children who can cope with the length and the variety of riding, but it is maybe not the one to do first in its entirety. You can always try sections. There's a car park at the base of Ditchling Beacon if you want to cycle Underhill Lane in either direction.

making a day of it
Ditchling Museum is a short walk (and signed) from Ditchling High Street. It houses a selection of works from the famous artists and crafts people that have lived in Ditchling, exhibitions and a family-friendly 'Art Explorers' trail for 4–12 year olds.

food and drink
Hassocks Golf Club offers tea, coffee and food. **Carol's Café**, on the East side of Hassocks station, serves delicious home-cooked fare (closed Sundays). A variety of Ditchling stops are mentioned in Route 9 (page 61).

bottom of the Downs Area of Outstanding Natural Beauty where the views should distract you from any hard work your legs are doing on those short ups and downs. Approach the base of Ditchling Beacon (nature reserve) and car park. Cross Beacon Road and continue along Underhill Lane. Ignore the bridleway down Nye Lane.

5 Cycle **L** at the purple restricted bridleway sign. Enjoy the secluded ambience of this short stretch of lane. Keep left by Witton House, heading down a mud and stone bridleway. By the pond, turn **R**. Keep cycling, enjoying the woodland wildlife.

6 At the fork, go **R**, following the Ditchling Link Bridleway sign. Watch out for the wooden steps. Come out in Nye Lane by the garage and cross almost **SA** into East End Lane. Dawdle along, taking the chance to admire these houses with a quintessential English village feel (think Milly-Molly-Mandy).

NB: At the end of East End Lane, look left for the footpath off the High Street to Ditchling Museum.

Go **R** along a tiny stretch of Ditchling High Street.

7 Turn **L** into Boddingtons Lane. Please dismount to push along this footpath but it's worth it to avoid the busy centre of Ditchling. At the end, turn **R**, jump on your bike and power up Lodge Hill Lane. The lane changes into a muddy track. Keep going until you emerge at Oldlands Mill, built circa 1703.

8 Turn **R**, passing Oldlands Mill House. Look for the wooden waymarker. You must take the right fork that is the bridleway, proving once again that where you want to go and where you have to go are occasionally two separate things. Concentrate to balance on this narrow woodland bridleway. Keep **SA** where the bridleway becomes compacted stone. Look out for the glinting mosaic effect and sharp edges where someone has laid tile fragments to improve the surface.

9 Turn **R** into Ockley Lane. It's a minor road but traffic is nigh on constant. Cycle about 1½km, ignoring two road turn-offs on your left as you come into Burgess Hill.

10 By the warning signs for the roundabout and school, turn **L** down the bridleway (if you reach the mini-roundabout, you've gone too far). Whizz along this recently resurfaced bridleway, cross Oak Hall Park and continue **SA**. Bear left and follow the bridleway. You're not too conscious of the railway track on your right, perhaps because it's hidden in the cutting. Keep right, cross the railway bridge and ride on, passing Nightingale Lane Meadows.

11 Turn **L** to complete this ride back to the Friars Oak. You'll be riding on the cycle path adjacent to the A273 but this time you won't notice the road, you'll just be pleased that it's downhill.

WOODLAND AND DOWNS LINK

NUTHURST // MAPLEHURST // COPSALE

ROUTE 14 // 15.3km (9.5 miles)

Our favourite thing about this route is the outstanding woods at the start. You can't help but feel the demands of everyday life drift from your shoulders as you cycle through these elegant and peaceful trees. Some of the climbs may leave you out of breath but let's face it, you can't beat cycling downhill through woods and most of the ups on this ride are either short or not too steep.

This route is hard enough to be challenging but not so tough that it puts you off. It feels quite adventurous, offering you the opportunity to ride through some tucked-away countryside on a good mix of surfaces, including a pleasant stretch of the Downs Link and some quiet lanes. Incidentally, you also ride past a real mix of rural abodes and a couple of very appealing pubs.

It's probably worth pointing out that the soil hereabouts is heavy Wealden clay and when wet, it sticks horribly to your tyres, gears and brakes making it heavy and difficult to ride. Generally, the rest of the ride is easy so you can relax, freewheel (well, maybe some of the time) and even have a gander at how the other half live. You'll know where we mean when you cycle through the grounds... don't worry, you can't miss it. In a nutshell then: Nuthurst, a mini adventure for only a medium-sized amount of effort.

Your starting point is near The Black Horse pub in Nuthurst. Use their car park if you're planning on taking refreshment there but do let them know what you're doing. Otherwise, there's plenty of parking thereabouts on the road.

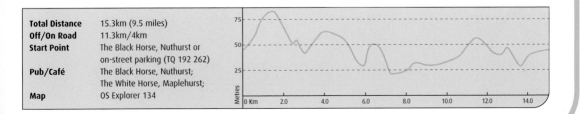

Total Distance	15.3km (9.5 miles)
Off/On Road	11.3km/4km
Start Point	The Black Horse, Nuthurst or on-street parking (TQ 192 262)
Pub/Café	The Black Horse, Nuthurst; The White Horse, Maplehurst;
Map	OS Explorer 134

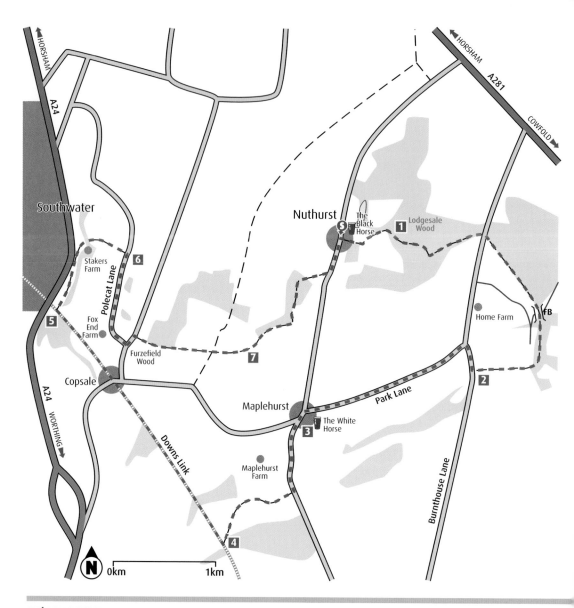

Southwater

Nuthurst

The Black Horse

Lodgesale Wood

1

Stakers Farm

6

Polecat Lane

Home Farm

FB

5

Fox End Farm

Furzefield Wood

7

2

Park Lane

Copsale

Maplehurst

The White Horse

3

A24 WORTHING

Downs Link

Maplehurst Farm

Burnthouse Lane

4

HORSHAM

A24

HORSHAM

A281

COWFOLD

N

0km   1km

Leave the pub car park and turn **L** onto the road. Turn **L** again almost immediately following the public bridleway towards Architectural Plants. Ignore the footpath after the plant centre and keep riding on the tarmac bridleway. The bridleway reaches the entrance to a house where you might spot a small sign for The Linen Shop. Here you must follow the wooden bridleway sign **R** (there isn't really anywhere else you could go unless you wanted to try and buy a bale of towels). Ride past the barns, keeping right as you stay on the bridleway. Ride up the slope towards the house.

1 As you approach the house, ride **R** along the bridleway into Lodgesale Wood. Cycle through the pine trees and bracken. This woodland bridleway is worth the effort any slight uphill stretches demand and there are some good views over fields at the top too.

Keep following the track along and around to where it narrows and runs along the side of the cottage bordered with white markers. Ride **L** along the tarmac road passing in front of Hop Gardens Cottage. Immediately after the cottage, turn **R** and cycle along the bridleway.

Keep **R** at the fork following the wooden bridleway sign. At the following wooden bridleway sign make a **R** turn. This is a good stretch to belt down because then you might not notice the impending uphill. See Home Farm buildings on your right as you cycle towards the gate.

2 At the junction turn **R** onto Burnthouse Lane. Pass Green Acres Farm and Redgates Nursery. Cycle **SA** on what will soon become Park Lane, past an eclectic mix of houses. At the end of the road, why not pop into The White Horse pub if you're thirsty?

bike hire
Cycle on the Downs Link from Southwater to join the route at Copsale.

family riding
This would be a good ride for active teenagers who like off-road as there is very little traffic to contend with.

food & drink
The Black Horse, Nuthurst is a 17th Century, listed country free house with good food and real ales.

The White Horse, Maplehurst, has been North Sussex's CAMRA Pub of the Year and stocks several different beers including JB Cider which is brewed in Maplehurst itself.

3 Ride **L** at the T-junction towards Partridge Green. Pass Maplehurst Farm and power up the steep hill. As you start to descend and before the road curves to the left, leave the road to follow the wooden sign **R** onto the compacted stone bridleway. Go through the gate and cycle **SA** along the edge of the farmyard following the bridleway sign. Follow the narrow track that runs between two fences. At the end of the fence, ride to your left, passing through into the next field. Cycle **SA** past the wooden waymarker. Ride diagonally left across the field following the bridleway past the electricity pylon.

4 Cycle under the old railway bridge and turn **R** up the slope (doubling back on yourself) to join the Downs Link. Ride towards Copsale and enjoy this easy stretch of the Downs Link. At The Bridge House pub, stop for a drink or continue over the lane **SA** on this old railway trail.

5 Leave the Downs Link before the tunnel which passes under the A24 and cycle **R** on the green-signed bridleway. The A24 is now on your left. The bridleway continues through Stakers Farm. Follow the wooden bridleway sign through the gate. Turn **R** just past the outbuilding and go through the metal gate on your left.

The bridleway here has recently changed course and is now well-signed. Ride over the bridge and follow the direction of the wooden waymarked bridleway. The bridleway briefly joins a track and, where the post and rail fence starts, there's another wooden waymarker. Leave the track to follow the bridleway across the field. Ride across the concrete bridge. This path can become churned up by horses and is sometimes hard to ride.

6 At the junction with the lane, turn **R**. Pass Fox End Farm on the bend and reach the end of Polecat Lane. Turn **L** towards Sedgewick. Just before the bungalows, turn **R** down a bridleway. Cycle along the edge of the field, following the wooden bridleway sign into Furzefield Wood.

Go through the gate. Either follow the bridleway sign **SA** through the metal gate into the field where horses are often kept or (and this may be preferable as horses can be understandably nervous of unknown two-wheeled creatures with eyes on the front of their heads moving fast or even rather slowly) if you wish to avoid the horses, push your bike round the outside of the field to rejoin the bridleway at an appropriate place. Ride **SA** on the tarmac bridleway, through the buildings that include some stables. Continue **SA** on the grassy track. There's only really one way to go but there's a small dogleg to manoeuvre round. Cycle on.

7 Cross the black path and go diagonally **L**. Ride across the (small) bridge and continue up the left-hand edge of the field. Keep left, following the track through the gate and past the bridleway sign. Follow the stream, keeping left at the fork. The track emerges onto a field. Follow the edge of the field, looking out for where the track forks by the corner of the field. At the fork turn **L** and follow the wooden bridleway sign up through the metal gate and onto the field. Ride on and at some point soon you'll come to a wooden bridleway sign which can be pretty much described as being in a field. Keep riding, following the sign round the edge of the field and through a gate. Cross over a post and rail bridge.

At the fork, ride **R** and pass through the metal gate. Follow the bridleway along the edge of the field for a short distance before returning into the woods through a second metal gate (the left hand track at the afore-mentioned fork cuts out this loop but we're not sure if it's an official bridleway). Cycle **SA** on the bridleway until you must go through a gate. Ride around the edge of the field, heading for the house diagonally opposite. At the road, ride **L** past the school to return to your car.

forest way & HIDDEN encLaves

forest row

route 15 // 14.5km (9 miLes) or 17.7km (11 miLes)

This invigorating circuit is a little bit of Forest Way and a lot of off-road. Once off-road, the bridleways are almost deserted and the lanes used are very quiet. Forest Way provides a couple of miles of easy cycling to help you warm up before you veer off into the hidden network of bridleways and smooth-running lanes criss-crossing this enclave of rural tranquillity.

There are a few, slow and steady off-road climbs, which is why we're putting this one near the back of the book. If ground conditions are poor, you may have to make a choice: either push yourself or push your bike, but however you choose to do it, you'll be rewarded with some good views and a feeling of being far away from it all.

In the summer, there's a mid-route digression to a tea room. Or for those who want to add on some more off-road, there's an optional route loop you can tack onto the end.

Your starting point is the long stay car park at Forest Row Community Centre on the B2110 (NB: the short stay car park opposite is empty on Sundays and has toilets). The nearest station is East Grinstead. See the section on Forest Way on page 136 for details of an off-road, easy riding link to this route.

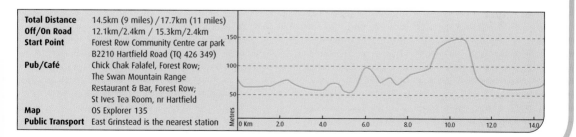

Total Distance	14.5km (9 miles) / 17.7km (11 miles)
Off/On Road	12.1km/2.4km / 15.3km/2.4km
Start Point	Forest Row Community Centre car park
	B2210 Hartfield Road (TQ 426 349)
Pub/Café	Chick Chak Falafel, Forest Row;
	The Swan Mountain Range
	Restaurant & Bar, Forest Row;
	St Ives Tea Room, nr Hartfield
Map	OS Explorer 135
Public Transport	East Grinstead is the nearest station

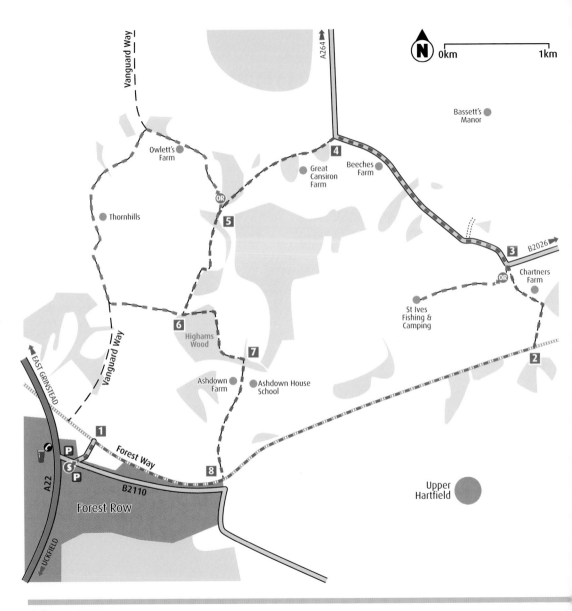

Vanguard Way

A264

Bassett's
Manor

N   0km   1km

Owlett's
Farm

Great
Cansiron
Farm

Beeches
Farm

4

OR

5

Thornhills

3   B2026

OR

Chartners
Farm

St Ives
Fishing &
Camping

6

Highams
Wood

2

7

Ashdown
Farm

Ashdown House
School

EAST GRINSTEAD

Vanguard Way

1

Forest Way

8

Upper
Hartfield

P

A22

S

P

B2110

Forest Row

UCKFIELD

Cross the road in front of the car park. Go to the left of the parade of shops and follow the track through the recreation ground. Don't go so fast that you miss the local 'shoe tree', the hows and whys of which are unknown. Go through some narrow, stripy bollards and turn **L** in front of the sculpture. Go over the bridge.

1 Turn **R** onto the Forest Way cycle trail. Cycle towards Hartfield, following the white arrows. You will soon fly past two old brick railway bridges but then you'll have a bit of a ride (approx 4½km) before passing beneath a third bridge (ignore any small footbridges which you must cycle over – only count the large brick railway bridges you must pass beneath).

2 After the third bridge, look for a waymarker showing a blue arrow pointing up to the left. Push your bike **L** up the old embankment and through the gate at the top.

Ride **R** down the bridleway, passing alongside the stream. Cycle over the bridge and through the pine woods. Ride up a hill, passing a small lake, signed Private Fishing and Shooting. Best keep your cycle helmet on. Pass Chartners Farm and continue **SA**. This narrow uphill track, where the central gully may be churned up by horses, presents a challenge. If you can ride up it, good for you. If you want to push, that's fine too.

3 When you reach the top of the hill, you have a choice:

Summer option: Take a detour along the lane to visit the seasonally open tea rooms beside St Ives Fishing and Camping. Ride **L** from the main route, passing Blackthorn Farm Stables as you stay on the lane. You'll need to pedal hard to get up the hill but, for once, it feels like the downward run is longer. Don't forget to keep an eye out for the camping and tea room signs on your right.

bike hire
Future Cycles bike shop and cycle hire is situated just a few minutes from our start point.

family riding
This would be a good one to try with teenagers if you are looking for something to challenge them. Younger families should stick with the Ashurst Wood Mini Mountain Bike Circuit and Forest Way.

food & drink
St Ives Tea Room, nr Hartfield – open in the summer.

Chick Chak Falafel – Healthy fast food! Truly delicious with a choice of sauces and meals. Spot the mobile green kiosk in Forest Row or check out www.chickchakfalafel.co.uk

The Swan Mountain Range Restaurant & Bar, Forest Row – uses 'hot rocks' to cook food in a 'mountain' setting.

making a weekend of it
Try camping at St Ives Farm, Hartfield. You could do this route straight from your front guy ropes and use Forest Way to explore farther afield.

See www.ukcampsite.co.uk.

Booking essential for summer weekends.

Back on the main route, at the top of the hill ride **SA** down the lane. Turn **L**. Ride down the hill, enjoying the smooth road surface. Pass the entrance to Bassett's Manor on your right. Keep swooping downhill, climb some more, downhill again and of course, more up too. Pass Beeches Farm on your left.

4 Where the lane turns sharp right (Cansiron Lane), cycle **L** towards Great Cansiron Farm, following the stone bridleway marker. Ride through the houses and follow the track past the outbuildings. Follow the bridleway sign **SA**. Make the slow climb, distracting yourself with the far-reaching views over the fields. Ride (or push) your way into the woods and follow the unmarked path. Eventually, the track runs in front of a house and joins another bridleway.

5 Ride **L** along the leafy bridleway. Pass two dead trees on your right. There's a local rumour that they were once struck by lightning. Follow the bridleway as it wends its way between trees and around the border of the fields. This section is slightly uphill and on soft ground.

Optional Route (adds approx 3km off-road):

At Instruction 5, ride **R** through the five-bar gate. Look out for the surface underfoot. Somebody has spent hours embedding bricks on their sides to improve the surface and drainage of this track but they wouldn't be any fun to fall on. Concentrate and don't let the breath-taking views across the valley towards the hay barn and the distant chapel distract you. Watch out for the steep descent into the farmyard of Owlett's Farm. You don't want to end up arriving sooner than you expected, flipping over the gate at the bottom instead of stopping to open it.

Pass **SA** through two more farm gates and notice the intriguing sculpture in the garden of Owlett's Farmhouse. This valley has a tranquil but friendly feel to it. Cycle up through the middle of the farm buildings at your own pace.

The lane levels out. Pass the well-named Dog Gate House on your left and Dog Gate Lodge on your right. Notice where the bridleway is signed **L** and turn to cycle along Vanguard Way. This part of the ride is gently uphill. Pass Songhurst on the left. Enjoy a short bumpy freewheel before another slight uphill. Pass Hurstbrook House and Thornhills on your left. Hear the gravel crunch under your wheels as you ride between the post and rail fences towards Homefield Cottage. Turn **L**. Keep following the bridleway. Pass Blackberry Hill Farm on your right and Orchard Cottages on your left. Rejoin the main route at Instruction 6.

6 At the corner by the transmitting station, cycle **L** (or **SA** if rejoining from the **OR**) following the blue bridleway sign. Ride into Highams Wood. This bridleway is occasionally closed due to excess water affecting the surface, although if you walk your bike down it, you may find it hard to understand why. Perhaps it relates to a couple of sudden dips and stone boulders that could be potentially dangerous.

This rooted, stony track runs downhill yet the lie of the land means that you soon find yourself following a path around and through the tree tops. You emerge to fantastic views over the High Weald and Ashdown Forest. Slip or ride down the very steep grassy downhill. The surface improves half way down. Follow the bridleway **L**. Ride on until you reach the lane.

7 Cycle **R** through the bollards, following the bridleway sign. Ride up the hill and see Ashdown House School on your left. Enid Blyton fans might spot the sign All trunks to the barn please. Ashdown Farm is on your right. Sweep downhill enjoying excellent views across the fields towards Forest Way cycle trail. You're within striking distance of the trail but this route feels far more remote.

8 **Easy to miss:** Before you reach the bridge, as the road starts to rise, look for the metal gates where you need to head **L**. There's a short footpath beside the smaller metal gate along which you can push your bike back onto the Forest Way cycle trail where a **R** turn will allow your to retrace the first section of the route back to the start.

WOODS AND PONDS of the UPPER WEALD

SLAUGHAM // WARNINGLID

ROUTE 16 // 12.9km (8 miles)

These woods are simply stunning and the ponds, that are likely remnants of the Sussex iron industry, are the finishing touch to woodland with some great gradients. However fast or slow you choose to ride, there's a timeless feel to the paths. This mainly off-road route also has some great views over the Upper Weald.

The starting point near Slaugham is just a few minutes drive from the A23 but you'd never know it. Once riding through this woodland, you may not see a soul and if you pause to rest, it might even be quiet enough to hear the rustle of falling leaves.

You probably will pause to rest... We've put this route near the back of the book because there are a few sticky off-road uphill sections. But by now, you may have ridden all the previous routes and have become so incredibly fit that your leg muscles don't even register hills, only mountains. Hmm...not working for us...not yet anyhow...

Still, apart from a bit of mud, it's hard to fault these woods and the experience of riding through these trees makes the uphills well worth the effort.

The starting point is the car park at Slaugham Common beside the large pond.

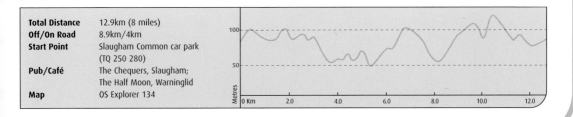

Total Distance	12.9km (8 miles)	
Off/On Road	8.9km/4km	
Start Point	Slaugham Common car park (TQ 250 280)	
Pub/Café	The Chequers, Slaugham; The Half Moon, Warninglid	
Map	OS Explorer 134	

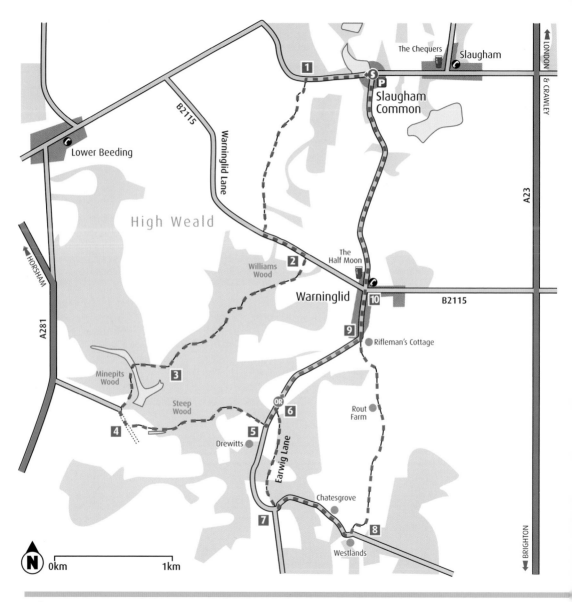

The Chequers

Slaugham

LONDON

B2115

Warninglid Lane

Lower Beeding

High Weald

1

S
P
Slaugham
Common

& CRAWLEY

A23

Williams
Wood

2

The
Half Moon

Warninglid

10

B2115

HORSHAM

A281

9

Rifleman's Cottage

Minepits
Wood

3

Steep
Wood

OR
6

Rout
Farm

4

5

Drewitts

Earwig Lane

7

Chatesgrove

8

Westlands

BRIGHTON

N
0km   1km

Cycle **R** towards Lower Beeding, enjoying the views across the pond.

1 Cycle **L** on the wooden waymarked bridleway signed Private Road, Gards Farm. Keep **SA** following the bridleway signs on this slow steady climb. Luckily, the ground surface is reasonable and what's more, there's a newly surfaced bridleway to whiz down on the other side. Come out on Warninglid Lane and cycle **L** up the hill.

2 As you start to descend, you pass some stone gateposts and directly opposite these, there's a right turn marked by a wooden waymarker. Go **R** through the metal gate and follow the bridleway to the **R** into Williams Wood.

Enjoy the downward run through the woods and turn **L** at the bridge. Ride up the short steep slope (if you can). This is followed by another down and a short up. At the top, enjoy the feeling of being surrounded by trees. Follow the bridleway sign across the clearing and cycle **SA**.

The bridleway runs downhill. Whilst enjoying this idyllic wood, do watch out for the embedded bricks and deep tracks that might catch you out.

Follow the bridleway sign at the post and rail fence. Cycle on along the bridleway past the next wooden sign. You may want to pause at the pond... carry on through the woods. The track runs alongside the top of the slope with a stream running down below. Keep cycling.

3 Push your bike **R** across the unusual stone slab bridge into Minepits Wood. Ride up the hill through the beech trees. We're glad this is a beautiful spot because we had to stop here to fix one of those never-ending punctures. You know the sort: you think you've fixed it but there's

famiLy RIDINg

Only if you have energetic teenagers who love the freedom of off-road riding and cycle uphill with a smile on their faces.

fOOD & DRINk

The Half Moon in Warninglid is brilliantly positioned near the end of this ride and welcomes cyclists. It serves ciabattas, ploughmans and a good selection of 'mains' beside the toasty fire or in the garden. It's also in The Good Beer Guide 2008.

The Chequers at Slaugham is ½km up the road from the start and boasts pub grub and real ales, although it is possibly not one for very muddy clothes...

a thorn hiding inside your tyre. Oh and another thorn. And another...

Moving swiftly on, watch out for the hidden rocks on your descent. This stretch can be boggy when wet. Follow the bridleway **L** and ride on, passing between the two ponds. It's likely that these ponds are remnants of the Sussex Iron Industry. You might see wallabies in the field on your right. Go around the metal gate and follow the bridleway **L** down the private road.

4 **Easy to miss:** cycle past the red-tiled house. Notice the old farm building converted into two garages; there's a waymarker opposite. Turn **L**, following the direction of the wooden sign through the gate. At the bottom of the field, go through the metal gate. There's yet another pond to enjoy. Follow the bridleway up through the trees into Steep Wood and yes, the name is a bit ominous.

On reaching the brow of the hill, descend, keeping **L** where the path forks at the bridleway signs and gateposts. Keep riding up through the pine trees. At the wooden waymarker, ride **R** following the stream when it appears. Continue cycling, bearing slightly **L** when you pass another wooden waymarker.

Keep pedalling if you can on this fairly long uphill stretch through rogue bamboos and rhododendrons. By the traditional 'laid' hedge, follow the bridleway to the **R** up a slight hill. The path forks shortly before the picket fence ahead. Follow the bridleway to the **R** and climb upwards. At the top, emerge from the woods at the entrance to Drewitts Farm, stopping to admire the smarter than average bridleway sign and the jockey on the weather-vane.

Go to the **L** of the Laurel hedge and ride onto the compacted chalk bridleway that offers views across the farm towards the trees.

5 Turn **L** onto the tarmac road.

Optional Route:
For a shortcut back to the start, stay on the road until Instruction 9 by Rifleman's Cottage.

6 Shortly after April Cottage, take the bridleway **R** into the woods and follow the leafy bridleway known as Earwig Lane. Stick to the bridleway until you emerge on a track that runs between red-tiled Deerhouse Cottage and white Bee House.

7 Turn **L** at the road and **L** again. As you pass Stonerocks Farm, look out for the plough on the roof of the barn. Enjoy the downhill, yes, downhill, run which passes a nature conservation area. This stretch of road undulates. Pass Chatesgrove with its various entrances. Cycle up the slope, passing the modern red-tiled house (currently called Westlands). Look to your left.

8 Ride **L** on the bridleway. There's a sign listing local houses, topped with the name Overhill. A hint of what's to come?

Cycle up the hill and follow the wooden-signed bridleway **SA** then **L** to the side of a five-bar gate. Cycle up past the field (owned by Sussex Horse Rescue Trust) enjoying views over the High Weald to your left. Pass through a gate and continue to climb. Continue through the gate and ride along between two fences that leave you no room to wander off-track. It's a hard camber to ride but, if you are able to build up some speed, watch out for the midway gates.

At the end, go through one more gate and turn **L** in front of Rout Farm barn and then **R** up towards the gate. The smooth surface of the bridleway makes for some easier riding.

Go through the gate and continue **SA**. You'll want to go fast on this smooth downhill track but, be warned, after a couple of speed bumps you turn the corner to find that the surface becomes craggy and pot-holed towards the end of the descent. The path rises up to join the driveway that in turn rises up to join the road.

9 At Rifleman's Cottage, join with the **OR** and continue up the hill past the Wealden House and into Warninglid.

10 At the crossroads, stop at the friendly Half Moon if you wish for a well-deserved break. Otherwise, cycle **SA** to ride the 2km back to the start. Look out for the WWII anti-tank obstacles by the small bridge.

WINDMILLS ON the SOUTH DOWNS

ROUTE 17 // 10.5km (6.5 miLes)

This route takes you up onto the South Downs, where you will find an enclave of rural tranquillity within cycling distance of Brighton. The circuit is more physical than some routes because it involves many ups and downs with virtually no level sections, and the majority of the route is off-road. The surfaces can be rugged and more hazardous so you do need to look where you're going. Not always easy because the views – and the feeling of being on top of the world – make you want to relax and soak up the charm of this Area of Outstanding Natural Beauty.

We've chosen to start the route at the Jack and Jill windmills in Clayton. The windmills are signed off the A273 and there's a sizeable car park with views onto Wolstonbury Hill to the west.

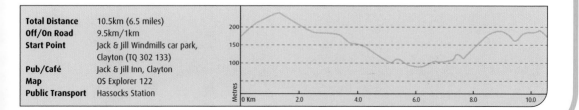

Total Distance	10.5km (6.5 miles)
Off/On Road	9.5km/1km
Start Point	Jack & Jill Windmills car park, Clayton (TQ 302 133)
Pub/Café	Jack & Jill Inn, Clayton
Map	OS Explorer 122
Public Transport	Hassocks Station

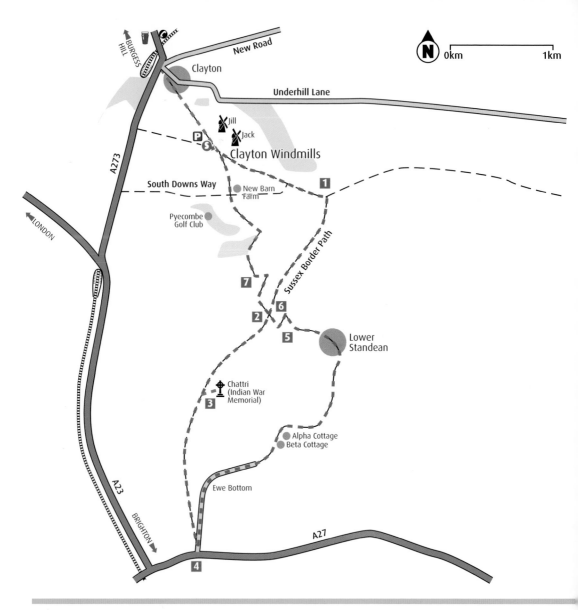

New Road

Clayton

Underhill Lane

BURGESS HILL

Jill

Jack

P

S

Clayton Windmills

A273

South Downs Way

New Barn Farm

1

Pyecombe Golf Club

LONDON

Sussex Border Path

7

6

2

5

Lower Standean

Chattri (Indian War Memorial)

3

Alpha Cottage
Beta Cottage

Ewe Bottom

A23

BRIGHTON

A27

4

N

0km

1km

From the car park, turn **L** up the flint and dirt track. At the signed fork, follow the South Downs Way towards the top. Don't be put off by this first uphill – we think it's the worst. Maybe that's just because it's a shock to the system...

Continue **SA** through the gate, ignoring the bridleway on the right. The last stretch of this flint and mud track has a gentler gradient. Pass three small windswept trees to your right and enjoy distant views towards Brighton and the sea. At the top of the hill, look along the hedge for a wooden post with blue bridleway signs. It's easy to miss and if you come to another gate, you've gone too far.

1 Follow the bridleway **R** (the Sussex Border Path), heading over the field before enjoying a bumpy descent. Look out for sparrowhawks. This downward slope is fun but you'd be well advised to close your mouth as you cycle; there's far too much flying sheep dung for our liking. Oh and watch out for the rocks and the kamikaze sheep too. The descent does become easier but don't be embarrassed if you let out a few squeals when you hit rough ground. No-one will hear you (well, except your mates). Try to keep your balance and avoid unexpected swerves due to the 'dung fly in the eye' syndrome. Maybe that's why some cyclists wear goggles... Go through the gate and **SA** down the next field. This one is much smoother and easier to ride.

2 You should come to a point where bridleways cross (this is the central section of our figure of eight route and you will return past this point later). For now, carry **SA** on this mud track enjoying views of grazing fields to your right and arable farm land to your left.

Local knowledge

Take a look at the **Chattri War Memorial**. It's dedicated to the memory of all the Hindu and Sikh soldiers who served in the Great War and died in hospital in Brighton. The memorial has an incredible position overlooking vast swathes of the Downs and, particularly if you are there alone, there's something very atmospheric about it.

The **Jack & Jill Windmills** are the only twin windmills left standing in Sussex. Jill, a white post mill, was built c.1821 and began life in Brighton but in order to harness more wind, it was decided to move her to a more open position on the Downs around 1852. Jack, a brick tower mill, was the home of writer and archaeologist, Edward Martin, for three years. In Life in a Sussex Windmill he portrays life in an old mill high on the Downs.

3 Reach a gate.

NB: Turn **L** to take a look at the Chattri War Memorial

Continue **SA** on the bridleway that runs alongside the fence. Enjoy the run, keeping an eye out for large flints. Look back towards the Chattri to appreciate the magnificence of its position. Ignore the gate on your right and cycle to the telephone pole and gate at the bottom of the field. Go through this gate marked No. 41, Chattri and Windmills, Downs on your Doorstep and continue **SA**. Enjoy the bumpy but fairly painless descent. You feel on top of the world with the rooftops of Brighton in the distance and only cows for company up here on the Downs. Do your best to ignore the A27: we all use it but it's only when you see it from a Downland vantage point that you realise just how it carves through the landscape.

4 At the bottom of the field, go through a gate and turn sharp **L**, doubling back on yourself for a short distance. It's a short uphill on a smooth surface and you'll be at the top before you know it. Keep **SA**. The bridleway sweeps downhill. Take care to avoid the significant potholes. Pass sheep pens on the left and enjoy the moment; you are now riding through a dip called Ewe Bottom. The lane climbs past Alpha and Beta Cottage, dips and climbs once more.

Continue **SA**. The track becomes flinty and uneven as you pass through the only place in Lower Standean. Use a low gear and keep climbing. Pass through the middle of the farm, keeping to the bridleway. Ignore any offshoots from the lane and head onwards and upwards. Pass a rough sand school without any sand and cycle towards the waymarker near the brow of the hill. It is marked No. 10 on the Downs on Your Doorstep trail.

5 The track curves to your right as you continue to cycle (or push, no shame in pushing...) your bike upwards. Spot marker post No. 11 on your right and ride past a flint and brick outbuilding. At the top of the hill, pass through the gates and take a sharp **L**. Follow the deep-grooved track up the side of the field.

6 You are back at the crossover point of our figure of eight route. Don't turn right, (the way you came) but cycle **SA**. Your hard work will be rewarded with a downhill soon...

On reaching a gate, follow the bridleway **R** between two wire fences. At the end of this section, go through another gate and turn **L**. You can see Wolstonbury Hill ahead and the windmills are diagonally right, which, by the by, is where you want to be heading. To reach the windmills, follow the track along the edge of the field and you'll see a track coming across the field at right angles to you.

7 Take the track **R** leading across the field. There's a waymarker on your left but it's easy to miss. It must be about time for a downhill... take it steady though because it's steep and rocky. The track curves around to the left passing the 10th hole on Pyecombe Golf Course. Once upon a time, the pond was the green but one year it flooded and now it eats unlucky golfers' balls. Moving on quickly up the hill...

Climb and climb some more. Push if you want to. This bridleway is narrow and uneven in places. Follow the South Downs Way **SA** (see wooden waymarker at crossroads). Go through the gates and cycle along the bridleway through New Barn Farm, before one last gradual (shortish) climb to the windmills. You're almost there. There's a surprise downhill at the end although why it's a surprise, I'm not quite sure because you did struggle up it earlier. At this point you can go straight down to the car park, investigating the windmills on foot if you wish.

Optional Route:

Alternatively, our digression gives you the chance to take a closer look at the windmills and have a sheep's eye view of Hassocks and beyond before either lifting your bike over the fence and into the car park or carrying on down the steep hill towards the Jack and Jill Inn. Don't forget that someone will have to come back up to fetch the car.

To follow the digression turn **R** at the marker post before the windmills as you descend the hill. It's a narrow entrance between two posts. Follow the track around. Your line of view opens out, extending over Hassocks and Keymer with Burgess Hill and even the North Downs in the distance. Spot Oldlands Mill, a fixture of our Hassocks route, on the opposite horizon. On a good day, the views are far-reaching. Come to a gate. You can see the car park on your left and the only way to get your bike back to it, is to lift it over the fence.

Or for the brave and foolhardy... the **Jack and Jill Inn** is the yellow building at the bottom of the hill on the main road. The energetic can cycle down the hill for sustenance. You will need something to eat before you come back up again! Follow the steep bridleway down towards Clayton. Watch out for the mid-point gate. The bridleway comes out on Underhill Lane near the church. Turn **L** onto Underhill Lane and then **R** on to a very short stretch of a rather hazardous and busy road to reach the pub.

WOODS, GREENS AND A WINDMILL

DIAL POST // BARNS GREEN // DRAGONS GREEN

ROUTE 18 // 23.5km (14.5 miles)

The lane sections of this ride are easy: uphills are short and downhills are long or maybe it just feels that way in comparison to the off-road. Not that the off-road is particularly hilly...more soggy and bumpy but fun nevertheless.

This route takes you through some fantastic woodland, past some choice pub doorways and you can even stop at a windmill with a literary past. Choose carefully whether you do this route in wet or dry conditions but whenever you do it, we'd recommend it either for a long and lazy ride or a fast-spin challenge.

Your starting point is in Dial Post, just off the A24. There's plenty of parking along the road. Anywhere within striking distance of The Crown Inn will do.

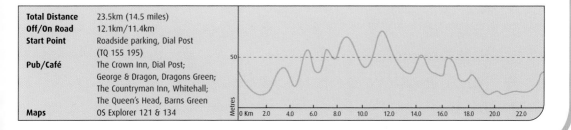

Total Distance	23.5km (14.5 miles)
Off/On Road	12.1km/11.4km
Start Point	Roadside parking, Dial Post
	(TQ 155 195)
Pub/Café	The Crown Inn, Dial Post;
	George & Dragon, Dragons Green;
	The Countryman Inn, Whitehall;
	The Queen's Head, Barns Green
Maps	OS Explorer 121 & 134

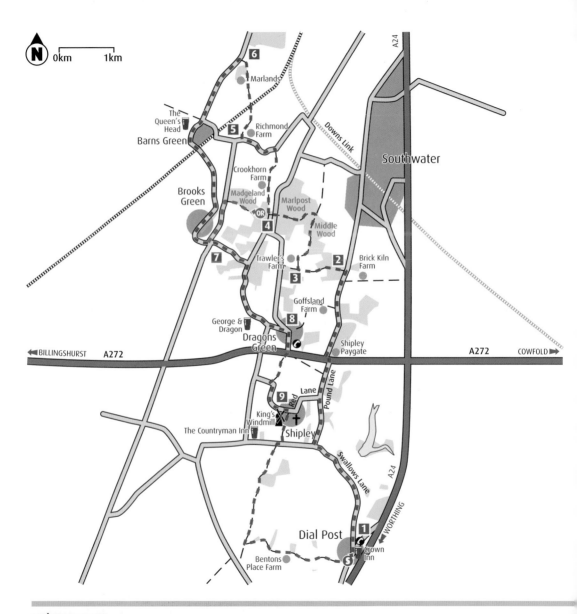

N 0km 1km

6
Marlands

The
Queen's
Head
Barns Green
5
Richmond
Farm

Downs Link

A24

Southwater

Crookhorn
Farm

Brooks
Green

Madgeland
Wood
OR
4

Marlpost
Wood

Middle
Wood

7
Trawler's
Farm

2
Brick Kiln
Farm

3

Goffsland
Farm

George &
Dragon
8
Dragons
Green

Shipley
Paygate

◄ BILLINGSHURST   A272   A272   COWFOLD ►

Red Lane

9
Lane

Pound Lane

King's
Windmill
The Countryman Inn
Shipley

Swallows Lane

A24

WORTHING

Dial Post
1

Bentons
Place Farm

Crown
Inn

Cycle along the road towards Shipley.

1 Ride **L** into Swallows Lane. At the white signpost, cycle **R** into Pound Lane. Keep riding **SA**, passing Red Lane on your left. At the T-junction, just beyond a house named Shipley Paygate turn **L**. Cross the A272 then immediately turn **R** onto Shipley Road following the sign for Southwater. Cycle **SA**, ignoring the footpath sign by the pylons and the bridleway sign at Goffsland Farm. Keep a steady pace up the slow hill. Ignore the bridleway to the right at Brick Kiln Farm. Pedal up the slow, steady hill.

2 As the brow of the hill levels out, go **L** down the bridleway before the post and rail fence. Cycle through Woodgetters Wood. Follow the bridleway through a gate and across the top of a field following the edge of more woodland. Follow the bridleway as it swings around to the right, down a slope, through a wide gap in the hedge and up the other side.

3 Ride **R** at the four way wooden waymarker. At the next waymarker, just after Trawler's Farm, follow the bridleway **R**, passing the barns on your left for a short downhill. Just round the corner, leave the main track to follow the wooden bridleway sign **L**. Go through a metal gate and cycle **SA**. Follow the bridleway round the edge of the field and go through a metal gate half way along the northern edge. Ride through the pine trees of Middle Wood.

At the clearing, turn **L** following the first wooden waymarker. Ignore the second waymarker but ride **L** at the third (**NB:** these three signs are very close together). Cycle along the undulating woodland bridleway through Marlpost Wood. Pass through a metal gate to the side of a larger wooden gate and on towards the road. Cross the road and cycle **SA** on the bridleway around the gate.

Local knowledge

Shipley Windmill is open the 1st, 2nd and 3rd Sundays of each month and on bank holiday Mondays (2–5pm). The windmill has at various times been known as King's Mill, Belloc's Mill and Vincent's Mill and has been home to at least two literary talents. The windmill was restored as a memorial to writer and poet Hilaire Belloc, who lived at Kingsland from 1906 to 1953. Scawen Blunt, a poet amongst other callings, lived at New Buildings and was known to entertain both Oscar Wilde and WB Yeats there.

The church behind the windmill was built by the Knights Templar, soon after they were given the land in 1139.

Don't be too put off by the sinking clay beneath your wheels on the first stretch; it does improve.

4 At the four way wooden waymarker, cycle **R**. I'm using the word 'cycle' loosely as this section can be muddy. Keep going until you reach a rough track where you cycle **R** and then **L** past 'chocolate box' Crookhorn Farm and pond. Keep cycling as the track leads you through mixed woods. At the road, ride **L**.

Optional Route (reduces overall route length by 4km):
At the four way wooden waymarker, cycle **SA**. This second stretch downhill makes for easier riding. Follow the wooden bridleway signs **SA** through Madgeland Wood. The surface underfoot improves to help you up the hill. Keep cycling **SA** past those bridleway signs. On reaching the road, cycle **L**. Ride on until you come to a fork. Go **L** towards Dragons Green, re-joining the main route at Instruction 7.

5 Just after the Barns Green sign, turn **R** into the lane, following the bridleway sign. Pass Richmond Farm Stables. Where the lane curves, you should see a wooden waymarker. Continue **SA** along the grassy narrow bridleway running alongside the hedge belonging to Rye Cottage. This bridleway leads you through woods and, in wet conditions, possibly a few puddles as well. One of Doctor Foster's favourites.

Cross the railway tracks with care and cycle onwards, following the bridleway signs **SA**.

You might want to push up this hill, depending on ground conditions. We did and we soon reached the top and were able to cycle on with renewed energy. The track

begins to run along the back of some gardens. Follow the bridleway signs **SA**.

6 The bridleway spits you out on to the road by Marlands. Ride **L**. Freewheel down the hill and straight through Barns Green. Pass The Queen's Head on your left unless of course, you're in need of refreshment. Cycle **SA**, over the railway crossing. Go past Cross Lane and a post box then up the hill. Pass Brooks Green Park on your left and a bus stop on your right. Keep pedalling. Pass another bus stop on your left this time. At the T-junction, turn **L** and then almost immediately **R**.

7 This is the fork where you are rejoined by the **OR** as you cycle towards Dragons Green. Enjoy the run down the hill and across the white-posted bridge, through the woods. Cycle **R** before the house that looks to be in the middle of a fork. At the top of the short hill, turn **R** again. Enjoy another downhill sweep, passing Dragons Stud on your right – a name well-suited to a fantasy novel – and later, past 1st Shipley Scout HQ, complete with thatched roof.

Cycle **SA**. If you fancy taking a look at the George & Dragon pub, now's your chance because you pass within waving distance of it.

8 At the junction with Dragons Green Road, turn **R**. Ignore the bridleway to the left. Ride on until you reach the A272. Cross with care. There are two bridleways here. You need to follow the one going diagonally right through the trees. Cycle **SA** along Boar Lane bridleway. At the road, cycle **L**, whizz around the bend and down the hill into Shipley. Keep riding **SA**, passing Shipley School and the Old Vicarage.

9 At King's Windmill in Shipley turn **R** onto the bridleway. See the church hiding to the rear as you pass close to the windmill. Cross two bridges and ride past a gate to emerge onto the road. Ride **R** and then almost immediately **L** at the first telegraph pole.

NB: If you keep on cycling along this road, you'll soon reach The Countryman Inn at Whitehall.

Follow the bridleway. You're approaching a section of the ride where if it's wet, you can't fail to notice the very large puddles; you may even land in them. Keep right at a fork with an unsigned footpath. Emerge at a clearing and follow the bridleway, passing a brick barn to your right. Continue **SA** through a gate. Keep cycling, ignoring all unsigned pathways on either side of the bridleway. Cross the footpath and continue riding for a short while. Look out for a wooden waymarker. Follow the bridleway **L**.

Keep following the bridleway signs **SA**. There should be a better surface under your tyres now. Ride through Bentons Place Farm and turn **L** at the wooden waymarker immediately after the large pond. Follow the bridleway **SA** for some time. The surface is reasonable (after very wet weather, this path works a bit like a bike wash; the only problem being that your feet get washed as well as your bike – great fun). You'll come to some houses, a Southern Water Treatment Works, some more houses and just when you think the bridleway is never going to end, you land at the road; back at the start.

farmLanD anD vilLaces, Boats anD traIns

CHaiLey // flEtCHING // BaRCOMBE

ROUte 19 // 27.4km (17 miLes)

If you are looking for a whole day out then this route is ideal. You could set off early and combine it with a ride on the Lavender Line or a row down the River Ouse from the The Anchor Inn. There are plenty of good pubs calling out for you to linger in their garden or warm yourself by their hearths. As we cycled the route, we fantasised about a summer's day when you had more than enough time to visit each and every pub you fancied...

Don't worry. One or two short sharp hills will soon bring you back to reality and there's plenty to see: farmland, rural villages, woodland, open views and if you're lucky, deer.

And how about the terrain? It may not be best-suited to wet conditions due to the nature of the ground underfoot but otherwise, it's the perfect mix of quiet lanes and hidden bridleways. A bit of everything and not too much of any one surface which is probably a good thing because it is longer than most of the other routes and your legs may notice the last couple of miles...

The starting point is in South Chailey on the A275. As you enter the village travelling north from Lewes, pass Swan House (previously Swan Inn) on your left and the Free Church on your right. The layby where you need to park is on the left opposite Grantham Close.

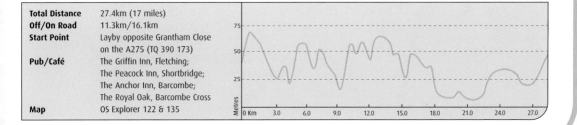

Total Distance	27.4km (17 miles)
Off/On Road	11.3km/16.1km
Start Point	Layby opposite Grantham Close on the A275 (TQ 390 173)
Pub/Café	The Griffin Inn, Fletching; The Peacock Inn, Shortbridge; The Anchor Inn, Barcombe; The Royal Oak, Barcombe Cross
Map	OS Explorer 122 & 135

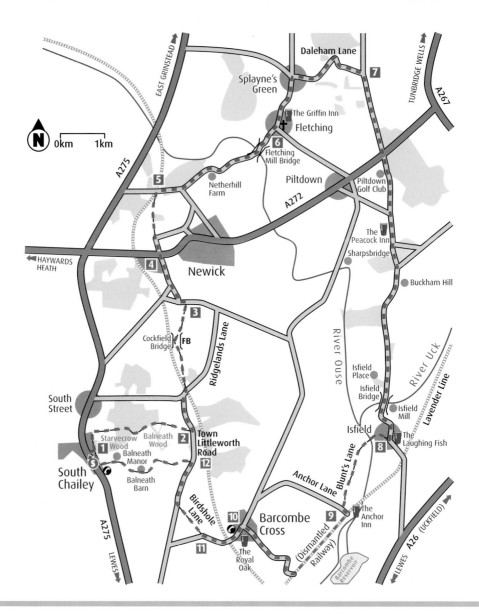

From the layby head north and turn **R** into Kilnwood Lane.

1 Cycle **L** at the point where the muddy bridleway runs across the lane. You may catch the aroma of iron filings... have a gander at the quarry workings as you cross the small bridge ahead. After the yellow and black warning barriers, turn **R** and cross the (unmarked) Greenwich Meridian as you cycle along Balneath Lane.

Follow the lane downhill through Caveridge Farm and **immediately** bear **L** at the fork onto the bridleway. Go through a metal gate and follow the bridleway straight ahead into the trees. At the clearing, follow Balneath Lane to the **R**. Pedal along this peaceful woodland bridleway through Starvecrow Wood and Balneath Wood towards the fields ahead. Turn **L** keeping the fields on your right.

2 Cycle **L** when you reach a quiet lane. At the junction between Town Littleworth Road and Ridgelands Lane, turn **R**. After a short distance, look out for the bridleway at the base of the hill. Follow the bridleway **L**. This woodland bridleway has a fairly good surface when it's dry but the same can't be said for wet conditions. Tackle the short uphill safe in the knowledge that the bridleway will be wide enough for you to enjoy the downhill. Watch out for fallen branches though and take it slow on the approach to Cockfield Bridge as there is a significant drop at the far side.

Follow the track **SA** alongside the wall where it can be muddy. Continue **SA** following the bridleway under the arched trees above and keep pedalling on the slow climb ahead. Continue **SA** past the gates to Cockfield House and onto a compacted stone track.

Local knowledge

The building which houses Isfield Post Office has the Cricket Club based behind it. There's been a cricket club here since 1758 and it's the oldest club in the county.

Although it is shown on the O.S. map as a pub, the Swan Inn is now a just house.

making a day of it

The Lavender Line, Isfield (www.lavender-line.co.uk). Take a ride on a steam train or just have a look around. Open every Sunday from 11am-5pm with trains every half hour.

food & drink

The Griffin Inn in Fletching is Sussex Dining Pub of the Year, with Harveys beer and rooms available.

The Anchor Inn, Barcombe offers good beer, high quality food and some magical rowing boats.

The Peacock Inn in Shortbridge and **The Royal Oak** in Barcombe Cross are also worth a visit.

3 Ride **L** when you reach the tarmac lane. Pass the post box and, at the white signpost, cycle **R** following the sign for Narrow Road. At the T-junction, turn **R** towards Newick. Go straight ahead up Oxbottom Lane.

4 Turn **L** when you hit the A272 but look immediately to take the **R** turn up Jackies Lane (almost opposite the junction) towards Headway Hurstwood Park. Ride down and then up, keeping an eye out for deer. At the top of the hill, we stopped to check our map and two approached us. This is where you leave the lane to go **SA**. You'll see a wooden waymarker pointing in the direction of Red Ghyll. Before the entrance to Red Ghyll, follow the bridleway through the wooden markers. The track winds down through the trees. Watch out for the bridge. You are now cycling through woodland attached to Little Warren Organic Farm. At the top of the hill keep **R**, following the bridleway.

5 When you reach the metalled lane, turn **R** towards Newick. After 0.5km, turn **L** into Mill Lane towards Fletching. Enjoy the smooth downhill passing Netherhall Farm and Bonswick Cottages. Pass the Mill House and stop on the bridge over the wide stream to watch the water if you wish. Ride over a second bridge soon afterwards.

6 Cycle on into Fletching, turning **L** onto the High Street at the junction. Stop at The Griffin Inn or buy a snack at the Fletching Food Company shop which is full of delicacies. Continue along the High Street, enjoying the superb downhill into Splayne's Green. At the junction, turn **R** and then **R** again into Daleham Lane. Ride along the lane enjoying the fantastic, steep-ish downhill that is followed by a sharp right turn/bend. Unfortunately, you must now climb back up the lane to regain some height...

7 At the top of Daleham Lane, turn **R** and follow the road for 1½km. Go **SA** at the crossroads towards Isfield, taking care as you cross the busy A272. Cycle along Golf Club Lane which bi-sects the course at Piltdown Golf Club. At the junction, ride **L** towards Uckfield. Pass The Peacock Inn on your right and later, Lower Morgans House Holiday Cottages.

As you pass over the bridge, the road veers left but you want to take an immediate **R** up Buckham Hill past Horse and Barge Farm. This hill is nasty but it's short and sharp. At the top, take a breather before turning **R** towards Isfield and coast along this mainly downhill and level road. Continue down the hill into Isfield, passing Isfield Place Farm and Isfield Place. Cross the bridge before Isfield Mill and soon reach Isfield Bridge as you cycle through the village. Isfield spreads out over quite a distance so you will have to ride **SA** for some time, ignoring several wooden waymarkers, before you pass Isfield Village Hall on your right.

8 You will find Isfield Post Office beside the cricket and football fields. It's housed in a utility-looking building. If you spot it, ignore the earlier house on the right named the Old Post Office. There's an **easy to miss** bridleway here. Look for a wooden bridleway marker close to the posts with red reflectors. Turn **R** in front of the entrance to Old Mill Barn.

NB: If you wish, cycle ½km further into Isfield and visit either The Laughing Fish pub or The Lavender Line.

Ride along the bridleway. Cross the bridge. Go through the gate and keep to the bridleway, cycling diagonally left across the open field towards the bridge ahead.

Go through the metal gate, across the wooden bridge and through the gate on the far side. Keep **SA** on Blunt's Lane bridleway with the River Ouse on your left. After a short slope, go through another metal gate to emerge from the trees onto a field. Cycle past the oak trees. Go around the WWII pill box, keeping it on your right to avoid the wettest ground. After the pill box, look right through the trees to find the track which runs **SA** along the hedge and fence. Keep riding **SA** between the hedge and the fence. Pass through a gateway.

Ride through the clearing, keeping **SA** with the hedge on your left. Ignore the gate to the left and the stile and gate to your right. Cycle along this grassy bridleway that is bordered by hedges. Upon reaching a small field keep to the right, until you reach a gate that leads you onto Anchor Lane.

9 Cycle **L** along Anchor Lane. Keep an eye out for occasional traffic. Look for the bridleway on your right, where rails are embedded in the road surface.

NB: Turn **L** to reach the food, Harveys and rowing boats on offer at The Anchor Inn. It's worth noting that this pub is very popular in high season and this lane is particularly busier at weekends as a result.

Manoeuvre your bike over the sleepers and past the gate. This track follows the path of a dismantled railway. Ride **SA** towards Barcombe Mills on the bridleway, ignoring any footpaths or farm tracks. Some sections have been coated with chalk to improve the surface. Towards the end, the sides rise up steeply. At the road opposite The Ticket Office, turn **R**. Follow the road as it curves up a steep hill. The views from the top give you a good excuse to both pause for thought and recover your breath. Continue on towards Barcombe Cross.

10 At the roundabout in Barcombe Cross, ride **L** past The Royal Oak. You may of course stop for a drink if you have the time, thirst and inclination. Otherwise, continue cycling across the bridge and out of the village. Follow the road around to the right passing the green painted 'Tin Tabernacle' building.

11 As the road bears left, take the bridleway leading off to the **R** just past the Sewell's Farm sign. Keep **L** at Birdshole Cottage, following the wooden waymarker. Follow the narrow bridleway to the right of the next cottage. Enjoy the seasonal dress of the trees as your wheels feel the ground along Birdshole Lane. Emerge onto the road and cycle **R** past Springles Farm. Continue until you spot Little Holman's B&B on the right.

12 You are aiming to turn **L** just past the two stone mushrooms on the verge at Harelands. Follow the easy-to-miss wooden waymarker through the wooden gate. At the next wooden gate, cycle **L** and ride onwards, enjoying the striking open views. Ride across the field and pass through a rusty gate. Cycle along the side of the hedge until you reach the end of the field. A ramshackle gateway leads into the wood. Go **L** almost straight away onto a leafy mud track that will bring you out at Balneath Barn Farm and a bit of welcome tarmac. Ride **SA**.

This smooth run takes you to the entrance to Balneath Manor. Turn **L** and enjoy this bridleway through farmland. Emerge through gateposts and at the white post on your right, turn **R** along the bridleway. Cycle along until you hit a tarmac bridleway crossing your path. Hopefully, you'll recognise it as the path from the beginning; it hasn't been that long a ride. Turn **L** and then **L** again onto the road to return to the start.

treetops, a reservoir and country estates

cuckfield // ardingly // borde hill

route 20 // 18.5km (11.5 miles)

Cycle up into the treetops, alongside Ardingly reservoir and through Borde Hill Estate. This route is good for fitness training because of the gradients. I won't tell you how many, but a lot of them go up and you certainly need your brakes in good working order. Carry as little weight as possible, so leave the picnic blanket and thermos at home. Not to worry, there are plenty of friendly pubs and cafés en route.

The route redeems itself in terms of the ground underfoot. It's almost all tarmac and even the bridleways are well surfaced. This makes it ideal for most weather conditions providing, of course, that you're visible to motorists. It's possible to join this route at Instruction 2 from Balcombe Station.

Your starting point is Whitemans Green. There's a car park at the recreation ground/football pitches off the B2115.

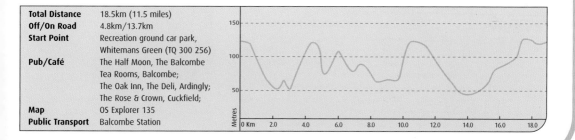

Total Distance	18.5km (11.5 miles)
Off/On Road	4.8km/13.7km
Start Point	Recreation ground car park, Whitemans Green (TQ 300 256)
Pub/Café	The Half Moon, The Balcombe Tea Rooms, Balcombe; The Oak Inn, The Deli, Ardingly; The Rose & Crown, Cuckfield;
Map	OS Explorer 135
Public Transport	Balcombe Station

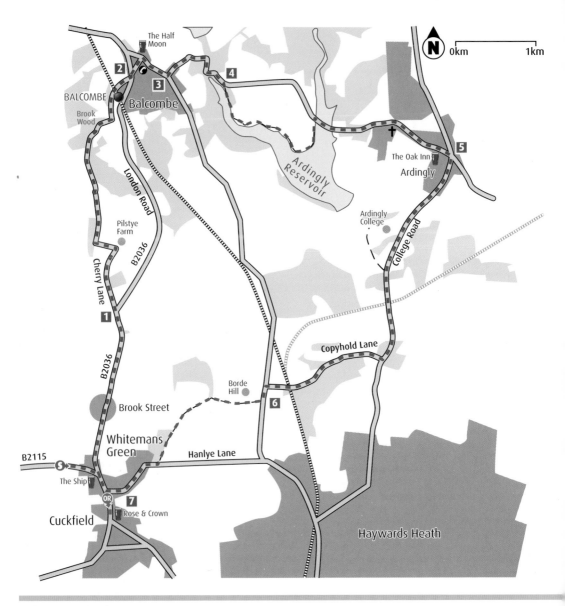

The Half Moon

2

BALCOMBE

Brook Wood

3

Balcombe

4

London Road

Pilstye Farm

B2036

Cherry Lane

1

B2036

Ardingly Reservoir

5

The Oak Inn

Ardingly

Ardingly College

College Road

Copyhold Lane

Borde Hill

6

Brook Street

Whitemans Green

Hanlye Lane

B2115

5

The Ship

OR

7

Rose & Crown

Cuckfield

Haywards Heath

N

0km   1km

Cycle **R** out of the car park. At the roundabout with The Ship Inn, ride **L** onto the B2036 (London Road) towards Balcombe. Cycle along this fairly busy stretch through the houses of Brook Street. Ride down the hill, enjoying views over the fields.

1 As the road rises, turn **L** into Cherry Lane, following the Sussex Ouse Valley Way for a short distance. Cycle along this undulating lane and pedal hard up the steep incline. Keep left where the lane forks towards Pilstye Farm. You'll know when you've reached the 'summit' because, looking back, there's a breath-taking view over rural Sussex towards the Downs. Or could it be your exertion up the hill has caused a lack of oxygen to the brain? Follow the lane along the ridge above the woods. Keep right as the road descends. Balcombe Estate is to your left. Enjoy the steep descent. Pass Brook Cottage on your right, cross the bridge over the stream and, where the track splits, cycle to the left. Pedal up the hill, under a railway bridge and uphill again. You can see why we put this one near the end of the guide...it's lucky you're now fit after cycling all those earlier circuits. Some of us might still prefer to push though... Pass the geese and the beehives. Breathe a sigh of relief as you reach the top of Rocks Lane.

2 **NB:** If you're joining from the station, head for Balcombe village and join the route below.

From Rocks Lane, cross the busy London Road into the road diagonally opposite (Bramble Hill), towards Balcombe. Cycle through Balcombe village and shops, passing The Balcombe Tea Rooms. The Half Moon Inn is at the junction. Ride **R** towards Haywards Heath, Lindfield and Ardingly.

LocaL knowLedge

Borde Hill Garden is a beautiful and botanically rich garden set within 150 acres of parkland. It was created in the early 1900's, the era of the great plant hunters. The Tudor mansion dates from 1580.

famILy RIDINg

This isn't a family route but for a child-friendly short and simple ride try parking beside the road at Instruction 4. You can then cycle along the bridleway and back, admiring the reservoir as you go. Adults could walk. Dogs must be on leads.

food & DRINK

The Half Moon, Balcombe offers freshly prepared home-cooked foods.

The Oak Inn, Ardingly, does home-cooking, traditional Sunday lunches and is highly recommended by locals.

The Deli in Ardingly is just past the bakers and has a couple of tables and, even better for those with tired legs, chairs.

The Rose & Crown, Cuckfield is a traditional, comfortable pub with garden.

The Balcombe Tea Rooms offers sandwiches, paninis, light bites, cream teas, Marshmallow Pavlova and Fruit Banana Split.

3 At the next roundabout, cycle **L** towards Ardingly. At Woodwards Farm, follow the road right. For those of you who like garden design, take a peek to your left. Now that's what you call a water feature. Perhaps a small project for the weekend? Ride up the hill. You're looking down on the woods from the other side now and can also glimpse the reservoir through the trees.

4 At the South East Water sign for Ardingly Reservoir, turn **R** onto a bridleway. Follow this stunning bridleway alongside 198 acres of water. Watch out for herons and sailing boats. Pass through the gate. Cycle **R** along the road, climbing into the treetops... on up into the clouds... past the graveyard and St Peter's Church. Continue **SA** into Ardingly. Stop at The Oak Inn if the fancy takes you. Don't miss the smells wafting in the air as you pass The Bakery, locally renowned for its delicious bread and pastries, cakes and fancies.

5 At the junction, turn **R** into College Road. It's probably worth mentioning that this can be a fast and dangerous stretch of road. Pass Ardingly College and Ardingly Reservoir entrance on your right. Cycle across the bridge and power up the slope.

Turn **R** towards Borde Hill Gardens into Copyhold Lane. This lane undulates but not as severely as those you've already conquered. Pass Copyhold Hollow B&B on your left. Ride over the railway bridge, past Cobwebs Saddlery and The Old Sawmills. At the end, ride **L** towards Borde Hill Gardens.

6 Turn into Borde Hill Estate through the first stone gateposts on your right, following the bridleway.

NB: You may wish to stop for a while at Borde Hill Estate to use the Café Elvira (open in summer). It's also possible to wander round the acclaimed garden and parkland (admission payable).

To keep cycling, follow the bridleway through the gate signed Garden Entrance. You will find this to the right of the roundabout. Ride **SA** along the well-surfaced bridleway, passing in front of Borde Hill House. Pass through the small gate to the left of the cattle grid. Continue for a short distance until another path joins from the right. Go **L**, keeping the post and rails fence to your right. Pedal onwards, admiring the views over the High Weald as you ride. Pass Stone Lodge with its stone gateposts. It's around this point that you start to wonder, "Surely I can't be pedalling up a slope again?"

Never mind, you've almost finished. Follow the wooden bridleway sign **SA**. At the gatepost, the bridleway meets Hanlye Lane. Cycle **R**. At the mini-roundabout, turn **L** onto Ardingly Road, passing the site of the old cottage hospital (which is now indistinguishable from a housing estate). When London Road is in sight, take a **R** into Brainsmead to avoid the traffic, followed by a quick **L** into Brainsmead Close.

7 Turn **R** onto London Road.

NB: Turn **L** to cycle to The Rose & Crown.

At the mini roundabout, ride **L** back to the car park at Whitemans Green.

railway trails

Railways changed the face of the land in Victorian England and like many other areas, the south east enjoyed an age of railway expansion. It is perhaps a good thing that not all the railway lines were kept open, as this has contributed to some areas retaining a greater rural character. Once the old tracks were removed, these abandoned lines were soon being used as an important wildlife corridor. In time, people too saw the potential of these pathways and several old lines have been officially adopted as recreational trails.

They are ideal for easy riding: no traffic, generally level (engines don't like hills either) wide and well surfaced. These characteristics make the trails ideal for child-seats, tag-alongs and of course children. In fact anybody carrying extra weight or gaining confidence on two wheels. The only drawback is that you must follow a linear route and double back on yourself. The advantage of this, particularly for young families or those returning to cycling after a long break, is that you can tailor your ride to suit yourselves: as long or as short as you feel like at the moment you decide to turn back.

DOWNS LINK

The Downs Link is an impressive 59km and for most of that distance it follows disused railway lines. There are small 'links' across the odd field or along a road but generally this trail offers traffic free, easy riding. The Downs Link does just what its name suggests: it links the North Downs Way and the South Downs Way. The trail was opened in 1984, with the final 5km being added in 1995 to link the seaside community of Shoreham-by-Sea. The trail begins at St. Martha's Weald, near Guildford, but we shall mainly concern ourselves with Stages 4, 5 and 6 as these pass through central Sussex. The route is too long to cover it all in detail but it's possible to download detailed map routes from www.mrcycles.co.uk.

You don't have to ride all of this trail in one go unless of course you want to... and if you're new to long distance riding, this trail is probably a very good place to start.

Distance:	59km (37 miles)
Map:	OS Explorer 122, 134, 145
Starting points:	The Downs Link can be started from a number of locations. We focus on Stages 4, 5 & 6 in central Sussex here.
Parking:	**Please use public car parks:**
	Stage 4 – Henfield: The A281 runs through Henfield. Turn off westwards into Church Street and continue into Upper Station Road. Park next to Downs Link, just beyond The Old Railway Tavern. Parking at **West Grinstead Old Station**, on the A272 opposite 'Springs' fish shop.
	Links: Route 10
	Public Transport: Horsham Station
	Stage 5 – Southwater Country Park: Approach on the A24 from Horsham or Worthing and follow the signs for Southwater Country Park. There's parking by the visitor centre in Cripplegate Lane where you join the Downs Link.
	Links: Routes 2, 7 and 14.
	Public Transport: Horsham Station
	Stage 6: Take the A2037 and A2038 to Steyning and Bramber. Various parking in Bramber, including the car park opposite the Castle Hotel. This is The Street free car park (with toilets!) Or park at Bramber Castle and walk back from the roundabout.
	Links: Shoreham Seafront Trail
	Shoreham-Worthing seafront trail: There's currently a small gap where road cycling is unavoidable but there's an application pending to join the Downs Link with the seafront
	Public Transport: Bramber or Shoreham Stations
Cycle Hire:	Southwater Cycles (01403 732561) has access onto the Downs Link at Southwater.
Visitor Information:	Southwater Country Park (01403 731218) has information, refreshments and toilets.

Stage 4: If you have small children, they may particularly enjoy the old station yard at West Grinstead. The old platform is still there, a signal and best of all, an old carriage which they can investigate at close quarters. There are several picnic tables and The Orchard Family Restaurant is beside the car park. This section of the Downs Link is mainly well surfaced and flat, with occasional, very short links across, for example, a field or along a short stretch of road. It's ride-able by almost everyone who has the fancy to do so because any such sections are very short and can be managed according to the needs of your party. The Bridge House pub is on the Downs Link at Copsale and there's a friendly pub, The Partridge, just over the bridge.

Stage 5: The stretch between Henfield and Bramber is about 8km and makes a good round trip with older children. The trail is a mix of tarmac and mud surfaces so is slightly more bumpy than Stage 4. As you arrive in Bramber, you pass through some quiet residential roads, emerging onto a track by Bramber Castle. There are plenty of places to eat in Bramber and Steyning but from the castle, you will have to cycle on several roads to reach them. Therefore, if your children aren't ready to cycle on a road, take a picnic.

Stage 6: The third section we're interested in takes you from Bramber to Shoreham-by-Sea. Turn **L** out of Bramber Castle, passing the roundabout, to join the Downs Link on the wooden signed bridleway. The marker is close to where The Street joins the roundabout. This bridleway follows the course of the A283. It is separate from the road but you do have to cross at one point. You then ride along mud bridleways until you reach the River Adur after which you continue cycling on asphalt tracks. The Downs Link currently ends in Shoreham-by-Sea. There are plenty of pubs or you could visit nearby 'art deco' Shoreham Airport café.

Local knowledge

Shoreham airport is more atmospheric than most. It's still a working airport for light aircraft with emergency services stationed here. The main building is art deco and has been used as a setting for several television programmes including Tenko and Poirot. The small museum has many interesting historical artefacts and there's also a café that comes highly recommended.

Bramber castle

You may picnic in the grounds of this English Heritage Norman motte and bailey castle (admission free). Built around 1070, the most prominent feature today is the remains of the Gatehouse Tower. There's space for children to run around and explore and plenty of grass to collapse onto. The children of William de Braose, starved to death by King John, are said to return to haunt the castle and 15th Century Lady Maud wanders unhappily. She was found dead after discovering her husband bricking up the dungeon that imprisoned her lover. Luckily the atmosphere at the castle today tends to be a little bit more light-hearted. There are no facilities at Bramber Castle but toilets can be found at the nearby car park in The Street.

forest way

part of national cycle route no 21

Forest Way is popular with cyclists at weekends and understandably so. It allows access deep into East Sussex countryside, an Area of Outstanding Natural Beauty. The trail runs from East Grinstead to Groombridge, passing through or near Forest Row, Hartfield and Withyham.

This tree-lined track takes you through countryside that could be a million miles from our busy day-to-day lives. The landscape is marked by small fields, scattered farmsteads and rolling hills, all of which may trigger images of days gone by. This track tends to be notably well surfaced and is generally flat. This makes it particularly accessible for people with disabilities.

Despite being a busy commuter line, Forest Way was axed from use in 1966. It was originally a continuation of the line from Three Bridges and today, it is still possible to link Forest Way with Worth Way.

family RIDING

If you're cycling in the direction of Hartfield from Forest Row, there's a good picnic spot. You'll quite quickly pass beneath two old brick railway bridges. Ride on for around 3km and before you reach a third brick bridge, look out for a pond on your right. There are wide steps down so you won't have to abandon your cycles and a couple of rocks to sit on. In summer, children enjoy dawdling at the water's edge.

Distance:	14.5km (9 miles)
Map:	OS Explorer 135
Parking:	**Forest Row:** The long stay car park at Forest Row Community Centre on the **B2110** (NB: short stay car park opposite is empty on Sundays and has toilets). Cross the road in front of the car park. Go to the left of the parade of shops and follow the track through the recreation ground. Go through some narrow stripy bollards and turn **L** in front of the sculpture. Go over the bridge. You are now on Forest Way. Parking is also available at Groombridge.

Cycle Hire:	Future Cycles (01342 822847) bike shop and cycle hire is a few minutes from our start point.
Public Transport:	East Grinstead Station (through Heron Tye housing estate) or Eridge Station
Links:	To Worth Way Railway Trail and Routes 3 and 15
Visitor Information:	Sussex County Information Centre (North) www.sussexcountry.com

worth way

part of national cycle route no 21

Don't be put off by the fact that Worth Way starts in the middle of Crawley. As soon as you're cycling along the track, you'll get that feeling of being out in the countryside. Railway embankments are a valuable habitat for many wildlife species and the trail reflects that.

In terms of accessibility the route's starting point in Crawley is a positive bonus as Three Bridges, a mainline station on the London to Brighton line, is a couple of minutes ride from the start. It also links with the 18km network of cycle paths that criss-cross Crawley. There are also various well-signed parking points from which you can choose to start your ride.

For much of its length, Worth Way follows the old railway line that ran from Three Bridges to East Grinstead. The line originally opened in 1855 and Rowfant and Grange Road (now Crawley Down) were the only stations en route. The line was later expanded to reach Tunbridge Wells but a century later the whole line was closed as part of the Beeching cuts in the sixties. You can still see Rowfant station, although it's not open to the public.

A small diversion from Worth Way will take you to St Nicholas Church in Worth. This Saxon church dates from the 10th Century and is well worth a look.

Distance:	11.3km (7 miles)
Map:	OS Explorer 134 & 135
Parking:	**Pound Hill South Playing Field**, Knepp Close, off The Pasture, Pound Hill, Crawley: From the car park, head left past the garages and along the track. Cross the end of the playing fields towards the 'embankment'. There are steps made from wooden sleepers ahead with a 'bike track' running up the side. Children love this but might need help.
	Turners Hill Road (B2028), Worth/Crawley Down.
	Grange Road, Worth
	At the end of **Grosvenor Road**, East Grinstead
Public Transport:	Three Bridges Station
	East Grinstead Station
Links:	To Forest Way
	To other Crawley cycle paths.
Visitor Information:	www.westsussex.gov.uk

seafront trails

We are lucky enough in Sussex to border the Channel. Cycling by the seaside means sea air and seagulls; bracing winds or beating sunshine; ice cream, cappuccino or warm beer on Brighton beach. It means something different for everyone but whatever it means for you, it's a safe bet that an hour's ride here or there will help blow the cobwebs from your mind.

Generally the coastline in Sussex is fairly busy. **Sustrans National Cycle Route 2** runs along the East Sussex coast. It takes in some cycle paths but also includes sections of busy road and is ideal for people wanting a long ride.

Seafront rides provide opportunities for refreshment, dilly-dallying on the pebbles, nipping into a museum or even wasting money on the pier. Don't forget to take a strong padlock so that you can secure your bikes while you head off to relax. Everybody likes that feeling of riding their bike to get somewhere and these trails provide you with

BRIGHTON

SHOREHAM HARBOUR TO BRIGHTON MARINA

The seafront at Brighton has a very special ambience. Colourful, idiosyncratic and cultural, it caters for everybody. There's a new sea breeze every day and there's always something fresh going on along the promenade. From the tourists to the day-trippers, the romantic couples to the dirty weekenders, the artists to the fishermen, there's people to watch at every turn and cycling along on your bike, provides the perfect cover for doing just that.

Locals often cycle along the seafront, either as a breezy shortcut to work or for pleasure and exercise. But there's no reason why non-locals shouldn't park up or come in by train, and use their bikes to gain a new perspective on Brighton. This trail runs from Shoreham Harbour to Brighton Marina. It forms part of **Sustrans National Cycle Route 2** and enthusiasts may want to continue on towards Rottingdean. Families may prefer the section from Hove to Brighton Pier.

The starting point is Shoreham Harbour. This area is interesting as it gives you the chance to pass through a working harbour and ride somewhere a little bit different. From the main seafront road, follow the sign for **National Cycle Route 2 (Hove 2, Brighton 4)** at the entrance to Shoreham Port. Use the pedestrian crossing if you wish. Go **SA** down the small road beside the Shoreham Port building. Follow the sign This way for the beach. Cyclists must dismount to cross footbridge. If you've never crossed the bridge before you won't mind dismounting to watch the locks work in the Harbour below you. If you're lucky, there will be fishing boats waiting too.

Proceed to the seafront. Explore to the **R** if you wish. Otherwise ride **L**, passing Carat's Café and Southwick Beach pay & display car park. **National Cycle Route 2** follows this quiet road, running behind the seafront pavement. Continue along Basin Road, an industrial road that joins this stretch of

Distance:	8km (5 miles)
Map:	OS Explorer 122
Starting points:	Shoreham Harbour, Hove seafront, Black Rock (nr. Brighton Marina)
Parking:	**Shoreham Port:**
	• Pay and display car park at Southwick Bathing Beach along Basin Road (behind Shoreham Harbour), accessed on main seafront road at traffic lights in front of Hove Lagoon.
	• Limited parking on road beside Shoreham Port building where trail starts.

	• Turn off main seafront road (by Optimum Appliances) and drive a short way up Grange Road, through the tunnel and find parking around the cricket green.
	Hove: Various parking along the seafront.
	Black Rock: Pay and Display car park (height barrier) at far end of Marine Parade, near Brighton Marina.
Play Areas:	Hove Lagoon (paddling pool)
	Kings Road playground (paddling pool)
	Nr Black Rock (paddling pool)
Public Transport:	Brighton, Hove and Southwick Stations

seafront with Hove Promenade. It's quiet at weekends but a short stretch is unavoidable which will make this part of the trail unsuitable for families with non-road safe kids (they'd be better to start at Hove).

At Hove seafront, a dedicated cycle path starts on the pavement in front of Hove Lagoon and runs alongside Kingsway. In sight of the King Alfred Centre, the cycle route diverts **R** down Hove Street South and runs along the promenade for a short while. The cycle path continues along Kings Esplanade before returning briefly to the promenade. The sea glimmers alongside as you pedal on your way. The cycle path continues along the pavement of the seafront road. Sometimes you're beside a grassy area, sometimes you overlook the promenade but often if you look right, you can see the beach huts or the sea.

You pass the Old West Pier, the site of the proposed Brighton i360 tower. As you approach the Palace Pier, you may want to dismount and investigate the Artists' Quarter. Here you will find craft and fine art shops, bars and cafes, a carousel and Brighton Fishing Museum. Basketball and volleyball courts may also be found between the two piers.

The dedicated cycle path ends in front of Palace Pier. If you wish to continue, you must ride along Madeira Drive. A lot of cars and coaches park along here so although traffic isn't generally fast, it is unpredictable. This section of the seafront promenade is geared towards a 'health walk'. Families wanting to continue might like to park and secure their bikes and jump on Volks Railway.

Pass the site of the first permanent beach sports centre and another play area. As you approach the Brighton Marina, you have various choices. You could dismount and walk along the promenade pushing your bike through the pedestrian tunnel into the Marina. Alternatively, continue cycling up Madeira

Drive and into the road tunnels. The blue signs for **Sustrans National Cycle Route 2** will lead you towards Rottingdean or you can cycle on the road into the Marina. It is worth pointing out that the return journey to Shoreham Port has a definite downhill edge to it.

seaford–
newhaven

The sea dominates the frontage at Seaford and the place
has a quieter feel to it than Brighton or Shoreham.
Backed by houses, the promenade is wide and simple,
opening onto a pebble beach and a wide expanse of sea.
There's a feeling of light and space.

The Martello Tower dominates the landscape at one end of
the beach. You can ride from it along Marine Parade, a fairly
quiet road parallel with the promenade, until the cycle
path begins. This section from the Martello Tower to the
Beachcomber bar is part of **Sustrans National Cycle Route 2**
which then diverts into town, rejoining us on the cycle path
towards Newhaven later.

Part way along Marine Parade, a cycle path begins. It runs
beside the road, rising up above the promenade. The track
offers good views over the sea and is an easy gradient to
cycle. The dedicated cycle path ends at the bottom of the

Distance:	4.8km (3 miles)	**Cycle Hire:**	Cuckmere Cycle Company (01323 870310) is at nearby Exceat/Seven Sisters Country Park. It caters for those wanting to ride to the sea at Cuckmere Haven or follow the mountain bike trails through Friston Forest.
Map:	OS Explorer 122 & 123		
Starting points:	Marine Parade, Seaford		
	Tide Mills off A259 Seaford-Newhaven Rd. Newhaven		
Parking:	Free parking along the seafront.	**Public Transport:**	Seaford, Bishopstone, Newhaven Town or Harbour Stations
	Buckle car park on the seafront road as you enter Seaford from Newhaven (toilets).		
	Also at Tide Mills.		
	Car park at Halfords/B&Q in Newhaven.		

slope by Newhaven and Seaford Sailing Club. You then have a very short stretch on the road (there's a narrow pavement here which children could cycle on).

The dedicated cycle path starts again at the entrance to the railway tunnel. The trail leads you out of Seaford, passing before the bungalows of Bishopstone. A short stretch of cycle path is right beside this busy road but soon the cycle path veers off to the left and is separated from the road by a grassy bank. You have views to your left over a small field towards the back of the beach and Castle Hill above Newhaven. Newhaven Fort is up there somewhere as well.

The path arrives at the gravel car park for Tide Mills "where nature meets history". Seaford Bay Exercise Path leads off to the left heading for historic Tide Mills Ruins and access to the beach at Seaford Bay if you fancy a picnic/sunbathe. The cycle path continues along the Ouse Estuary Nature Reserve. This nature reserve has been created by the council to make up for the loss of habitat and flood plain caused by the new business park and road. The area obviously provides a much-needed habitat for waders such as the little egret and the shelduck as well as smaller creatures like great crested newts. There are no bridle paths but cycles are welcome on tracks and, in dry weather, on the grass footpaths. The cries of seagulls and a gusting or gentle sea breeze will accompany the turning of your wheels as you ride on your way.

The cycle path continues past the reserve and into Newhaven, ending at the superstores. Adults who don't mind traffic may want to cross the swing-bridge and following **Sustrans National Cycle Route 2**; turn **L** towards Newhaven Harbour and Marina. Newhaven Marina was the first purpose-built marina in Britain. Newhaven Fort is at the top of Castle Hill.

SHOREHAM BEACH

LANCING // WORTHING

This trail is long enough to provide you with an enjoyable ride. It gives flat, easy riding and the opportunity to cycle along the back of the beach for a decent stretch. Light reflects off the sea on the dullest of days and the wind will either blow you along or give you a good workout. On a sunny day there's a definite hustle and a bustle around the beach huts. You can buy fish straight from the boat, as the day's catch is often for sale. This path can be busy at weekends and high season and you do need to watch out for dogs, old people and children. It's not the place to do a speed-cycle. If you ride all the way to Worthing, you probably deserve that cup of coffee and piece of cake. It seems almost criminal to waste a sunny terrace by the sea...

Distance:	8km (5 miles)
Map:	OS Explorer 121 & 122
Starting points:	Old Fort, Shoreham Beach
	Widewater Lagoon, Shoreham Beach
Parking:	Widewater Lagoon, Shoreham Beach, right beside the start of the dedicated cycle path, so good for families (height barrier, fee payable in high season).
	Pay & Display car park, Lower Beach Road opposite Waterside Pub (height barrier).Old Fort Car Park, Fort Haven Road (no height barrier!).
Cycle Hire:	www.m-cyclehire.co.uk offers mobile cycle hire covering central Sussex.
Public Transport:	The nearest station is Shoreham

OLD FORT

Shoreham Fort was built in 1857 when the appearance of improved steam warships fuelled fears of invasion. The fort never fired its guns in anger and was abandoned before the First World War. It took on a new lease of life when 'The Sunny South Film Company' used it as a film studio. In those days, there was no artificial light available and so the company relied on the good natural light of the fort's parade ground. Their name says it all.

SHOREHAM BEACH
Site of Nature Conservation Importance
The vegetated shingle is an internationally rare habitat and unfortunately, the survival of this unique wildlife community depends on people treating the beach with respect. Plants living in the shingle have evolved to survive the harsh, exposed environment and they provide a valuable food source and shelter for a diversity of insects and birds.

WIDEWATER LAGOON
This is a shallow saline lagoon, situated on marshland formed by sediments deposited by the River Adur. It's a significant winter feeding ground and haven for many birds such as redshank, grey heron, pied wagtail, kestrel, black-headed gull and ringed plover.

COLOURS ON PATH
Red: Dismount for short distance
(often where paths cross or for pedestrians' safety).
Green: Cycle.
Black with marked cycle lane: Stay in lane.

The point furthest east where you could start on Shoreham Beach is at the Old Fort. Have a wander and then ride out on Fort Haven Road and along Harbour Way. This road runs the length of Shoreham Beach passing a variety of houses.

At the far end, you will reach Widewater Lagoon. Families would probably be best starting at Widewater Lagoon as they can then ride straight onto the cycle path. The path runs along the side of the lagoon, past various beach huts, caravans and Lancing Sailing Club. It continues on into Lancing. Here a marked cycle path runs along the pavement next to a busy road for a short distance before veering back onto a track beside the beach.

Pass the Leisure Fun Park, which might be a good place for families to head for. There's a boating lake (algae permitting) and a small amusement park so if you don't mind bribing them to keep cycling, this might do the trick.

Or if a chocolate cake is more their kind of carrot, you could head on towards Worthing. The cycle path ends within sight of Worthing Pier. You can carry on along the very busy road or push your bikes on the promenade. Macari's Café, offers a good choice of basic fare such as cakes, a kid's menu, simple meals and ice cream cornets. There should be space to on the terrace prop your bikes up well within sight.

appendix

tourist information offices

Brighton	09067 112 255
Crawley	01293 846 968
Horsham	01403 211 661
Lewes	01273 483 448
Seaford	01323 897 426
Worthing	01903 221 066

bike hire

Forgotten your bike?

Cuckmere	Cuckmere Cycle Company 01323 870310 www.cuckmere-cycle.co.uk
Forest Row	Future Cycles 01342 822847 www.futurecycles.co.uk
Southwater	Southwater Cycles 01403 732561 www.southwatercycles.co.uk
Mobile cycle hire	M's Cycle Hire Maria: 07852 986165 John: 07852 986163 www.m-cyclehire.co.uk

bike shops

Burgess Hill	Anthony Hole & Sons T: 01444 233176
Seaford	Mr Cycles T:01323 893130 www.mrcycles.co.uk
Worthing	Quest Adventure T: 01903 573 700 www.questadventure.co.uk

weather

BBC	www.bbc.co.uk/weather
Met Office	www.metoffice.com

accommodation

Youth Hostels	www.yha.org.uk
Arundel	0870 770 5676
Blackboys, Uckfield	01825 890607
Telscombe, Lewes	0870 770 6062
Truleigh Hill, Shoreham-by-Sea	0870 770 6078

camping

www.ukcampsite.co.uk

Barns Green	Sumners Pond Fishery & Campsite 01403 732539
Hartfield	St Ives Camping & Fishing 01892 770213

cafés

Ardingly	The Deli 01444 891660
Balcombe	The Balcombe Tea Rooms 01444 811777
Ditchling	Chestertons 01273 836638
	Ditchling Tea Rooms 01273 842708
Hassocks	Carol's Café, Station Approach East 01273 841155 Hassocks Golf Club www.hassocksgolfclub.co.uk

takeaway food

Forest Row	www.chickchakfalafel.co.uk

PUBS

Details of most of the pubs we've mentioned are listed below, or visit: www.beerintheevening.com

Ardingly	The Oak Inn 01444 892244
Ashington	The Red Lion 01903 892226
Balcombe	The Half Moon Inn 01444 811582
Barcombe	The Anchor Inn 01273 401029 www.anchorinnandboating.co.uk
	The Royal Oak 01273 400418
Barns Green	The Queen's Head 01403 730436
Crawley	The Plough, Ifield 01293 524292
Dial Post	The Crown Inn 01403 710902

Ditchling	The Bull 01273 843147 The White Horse Inn 01273 842006	**Isfield**	The Laughing Fish 01825 750349
Ditchling Common	Royal Oak Inn 01444 471 263	**Maplehurst**	The White Horse 01403 891208
Dragons Green	The George & Dragon 01403 741320	**Nuthurst**	The Black Horse Inn 01403 891272
Faygate	The Holmbush Inn 01293 851539	**Plumpton Green**	The Plough Inn 01273 890311
Fletching	The Griffin Inn 01825 722890	**Rusper**	The Star Inn 01293 871264
Forest Row	The Swan Mountain Range Restaurant & Bar 01342 822318	**Shortbridge**	The Peacock Inn 01825 762463
Goddard's Green	The Sportsman Inn 01444 233460	**Thakeham**	The White Lion Inn 01798 813141
Hassocks	The Friars Oak 01273 847801	**Warninglid**	The Half Moon www.thehalfmoonwarninglid.co.uk 01444 461227
Henfield	The Cat and Canary 01273 492509	**Whitehall**	The Countryman Inn 01403 741383
Horsted Keynes	The Green Man 01825 790656	**Wineham**	The Royal Oak, Bob Lane 01444 881 252

places of interest

Animaline	01342 810596
Borde Hill Gardens	www.bordehill.co.uk
Ifield Water Mill	01293 539088
Lavender Line	www.lavender-line.co.uk
Newhaven Museum	www.newhavenmuseum.co.uk
Oldland Windmill	www.oldlandwindmill.co.uk
Seaford Museum	www.seafordmuseum.co.uk

other publications/websites

www.**v-outdoor**.co.uk
Cycling, mountain biking, walking and climbing books, maps and CDs

South East Mountain Biking North & South Downs
Nick Cotton, Vertebrate Publishing

South East Mountain Biking Ridgeway & Chilterns
Nick Cotton, Vertebrate Publishing

www.**sustrans**.org.uk
More info about the National Cycle Network

The West Sussex Village Book
Tony Wales, Countryside Books

about the authors

Deirdre Huston

Deirdre was born in Sussex and lives locally. She spends much of her time writing fiction and poetry and is often inspired by the creativity, enthusiasm and ideas of the children and young people at her Young Writer's Workshops (see www.youngwritersworkshops.co.uk for further information). A qualified teacher, she enjoys cycling and taking photographs – this guidebook has provided her with the perfect excuse to explore rural Sussex whilst doing those very things.

Marina Bullivant

Marina Bullivant grew up in Buckinghamshire and Berkshire. She worked in a variety roles in different industries before moving to Sussex in 2002 with her husband and two children where they embarked on a '10 year project' to renovate an old farmhouse. This was, however, completed within 3 years! She cycles for pleasure and fitness, enjoying being outside and is constantly on the lookout for new routes and tracks. Aside from her family, travelling, walking, the gym and reading, her other love is skiing.

vertebrate publishing

Vertebrate Publishing is one of a new breed of independent publishers, dedicated to producing the very best outdoor titles. We have award-winning and bestselling titles covering a range of activities, including; mountain biking, cycling, rock climbing, hillwalking and others. Our autobiography of British rock climber **Jerry Moffatt** won the **Grand Prize** at the **2009 Banff Mountain Book Festival** – one of the biggest prizes in publishing in the outdoors, environment and adventure genres. For more information about Vertebrate Publishing please visit our website: **www.v-publishing.co.uk** or email us: **info@v-publishing.co.uk**

Traffic-free family & leisure cycling in
Kent, Sussex, Surrey & Hampshire

Cycling Days Out

South East England

Deirdre Huston

Cycling Days Out

South East England

Traffic-free family & leisure cycling in Kent, Sussex, Surrey & Hampshire

Cycling Days Out – South East England is a guide to the fantastic family & leisure cycling on offer in East and West Sussex, Kent, Surrey & Hampshire, including the New Forest and the Isle of Wight.

Featuring detailed information on leisure cycling trails in England's beautiful sunshine counties, this book is an essential guide for all enthusiastic cyclists.

Each trail is described with:
- Detailed local area information
- Ordnance Survey Maps
- Local pubs, cafés and accommodation
- Information on easy access options for off-road wheelchairs, buggies and handcycles

VERTEBRATE PUBLISHING

Published by **Vertebrate Publishing**
*www.**v-publishing**.co.uk*

Mountain**Biking**
in South East England

Guidebooks from Vertebrate Publishing

South East Mountain Biking North & South Downs is a compact guide to the best riding on the Downs of Kent and Sussex. The area is criss-crossed with bridleways and byways - escape the towns and cities and explore the finest woodland and open chalk tracks while enjoying panoramic views of the Weald and the English Channel.

South East Mountain Biking Ridgeway & Chilterns takes in the best riding either side of the ancient Ridgeway and the Chiltern Hills west of London. Explore the Thames Valley, the Hampshire Downs and lose yourself in the Chilterns.

Each guide offers 24 routes suitable for riders of all abilities and features easy-to-follow directions and specially designed mapping, as well as details of distance, grade of difficulty, route profiles and local area information including refreshment stops.

find out more at:
www.**v-publishing**.co.uk